GW00871232

The line references quoted in this book refer to the
Gill and Macmillan edition of *The Plough and the Stars*.

GILL'S NOTES

The Plough and the Stars

SEÁN MOFFATT

GILL AND MACMILLAN

Published in Ireland by
Gill and Macmillan Ltd
Goldenbridge
Dublin 8
with associated companies throughout the world
© Commentary, Seán Moffatt 1991
0 7171 1834 7
Print origination in Ireland by
Seton Music Graphics Ltd, Bantry, Co. Cork

Contents

The Author

Seán Moffatt is editor of the Gill and Macmillan edition of Seán O'Casey's *The Plough and the Stars*. He studied and taught at Coláiste Eoin, Finglas, Dublin, and has directed and acted in numerous professional stage productions. He was artistic director of Trapdoor Theatre Company which toured Ireland with shows for schools and theatres. His one-act play *There is no Night* was awarded first place in the AIB sponsored play-writing competition and was performed during the Dublin Theatre Festival. Seán Moffatt is a regular contributor to RTE's radio drama for children and has adapted work for the BBC's education network. He has also written a number of adult plays for RTE and BBC. He has lectured on and given workshops in drama both in Ireland and Europe. He has written extensively for *Theatre Ireland Magazine* and contributed to radio and newspapers in his capacity as theatre critic. He is also the editor of the Gill and Macmillan edition of Seán O'Casey's *Juno and the Paycock*.

PART 1

Introduction

SEÁN O'CASEY

Every writer puts something of him or herself into their work: just how much can vary greatly. But a work of art is never created in a vacuum, and, as often as not, to know something of the author and his or her times can be of immense value in understanding and appreciating their work. Seán O'Casey is a case in point.

Born on 30 March 1880 at 85 Upper Dorset Street, O'Casey was the youngest child of a large middle-class Protestant family. His father, a well-read, scholarly man, died when O'Casey was just six years old. It was only after his father's death that the family came upon hard times, but by then his brothers and sisters were old enough to earn wages. It is true that O'Casey knew deprivation in these early years, but not, as is commonly assumed, utter poverty. His sister Bella became a qualified primary teacher, his brothers Mick and Tom acquired much-coveted positions in the post office as clerk and as sorter. Strictly speaking, by the standards of the time, the O'Caseys lived in relative comfort.

Though O'Casey was a sickly child, with a chronic eye disease which made formal education impossible, he none the less managed to learn how to read and write and became involved in bible studies, prayer meetings, foreign mission work, and teaching at Sunday School at an early age.

The city of Dublin was then fermenting with revolutionary ideas; O'Casey found himself in the thick of it all. Between 1896 and 1910, he was to progress from the non-political Gaelic League to the Militant IRB (the Irish Republican Brotherhood), both of which he eventually rejected in favour of the Labour Movement. His acute awareness of the poverty of those around him led O'Casey to a lifelong socialist belief. Disillusioned with middle-class nationalism, he concentrated instead on the labour movement in Ireland, being strongly influenced by James Larkin in particular. As an unskilled worker himself, his jobs varied from caretaker to builder's labourer. He joined the Irish Transport and General Workers' Union and rose in its ranks, writing for its newspaper and becoming secretary of the Irish Citizen Army. It was because of his antipathy to Larkin's successor, James Connolly, who was intent on formulating a common policy with the IRB, the aims of which were to free Ireland from British rule by force, that O'Casey eventually fell out with this movement also.

By 1916, when the Easter Rising took place, the thirty-six year old O'Casey had become disillusioned with, and had estranged himself from, just about every important movement and institution in the city. From then on, while still earning his living as a labourer, he concentrated all the more on his writing. He published a history of the Citizen Army and had his first four plays rejected by the Abbey Theatre before *The Shadow of a Gunman* was accepted, and eventually performed in 1922. In 1924, *Juno and the Paycock* opened at the Abbey and was so successful it had to be extended for a second week, which was something of a record for the Abbey at that time. For this, O'Casey received the princely sum of twenty-five pounds. 1926 saw the first production of *The Plough and the Stars*, which caused the most serious disorders the Abbey had seen since J. M. Synge's *The Playboy of the Western World*.

One of the strongest influences on O'Casey throughout that period had been his mother with whom he continued to live until her death. This would help to explain why it is that the most striking and most sympathetic figures in O'Casey's plays are usually the women, Bessie Burgess being the obvious example in *The Plough and the Stars*. In *Inishfallen Fare Thee Well,* O'Casey tells us that, 'She (his mother) had been his comforter, his rod and staff, his ever present help in time of trouble. . . . She was, in her bravery, her irreducible and quiet endurance, her fearless and cheery battle with a hard, often brutal, life, the soul of Socialism.' It would not be difficult to credit Bessie with much the same sterling, enduring qualities.

Arguably, O'Casey never wrote so well again after *The Plough and the Stars*. In 1926, he exiled himself to England where he lived and continued to write both plays and prose until his death in 1964. O'Casey was, in may ways, a stubborn, determined man. His anger is clearly evident in his work, but the rage is tempered because, fundamentally, he was also a profoundly generous, compassionate man who cherished, more than anything else, the ideal of a world bereft of poverty in which people could live together in harmony. These are the first clues we have to an understanding of the play. We will find O'Casey's anger, his pity, his optimism and his disillusionment, all the contrary aspects of his own personality, his beliefs and prejudices, expressed in different ways through the different characters.

APPRECIATING THE PLAY

O'Casey was forty-three years of age when he had his first play, *The Shadow of a Gunman*, staged at the Abbey after a number of other rejections. As the brief outline above shows, he had by then distanced himself from many causes, movements and organisations. By turning to drama, he tried to recreate an accurate picture of those troubled and turbulent times, from 1916 to 1922, as he had experienced them. It was his way of setting the record straight and, at the same time, of ridiculing and undermining those with whom he had come to disagree.

This is why O'Casey's life and times are so important in trying to grasp the full implications of his work. Yes, we may apply his wisdom to a broader, more universal scheme, as his work goes from the particular to the universal. But unless we fully grasp the particular, we can only half-understand the universal significance of the work.

This is why it is important to remember O'Casey's own disillusionment with the Irish trades unions and the Labour Movement when we come to meet The Covey; why we need to understand O'Casey's final rejection of an armed struggle against the British occupation of Ireland when we witness the confused patriotism and heroism of Jack Clitheroe. It is only when we understand that O'Casey was an intensely spiritual, at times mystical, person, that we can fully appreciate Bessie Burgess's ability to turn to God even when all else is lost. O'Casey put a great deal of himself—what he had experienced, lessons he had learnt, the people he came to value above all else—into his work. To know these things about O'Casey and the times he lived through is vital to an understanding of *The Plough and the Stars*.

THE SOCIAL CONTEXT

Jack Clitheroe's work as a bricklayer, The Covey's as a fitter and Uncle Peter's as a labourer would account for the fact that the Clitheroes are by no means destitute. Though they are clearly living in overcrowded conditions, by the general standards of tenement life at the time the Clitheroe household would not be typical. For the unskilled working classes, Dublin at the turn of the century was a city of extreme poverty, unemployment, poor housing conditions and a high mortality rate. A family such as the Clitheroes, with three wage earners and no children, would be the exception rather than the rule.

A rapidly expanding population served only to intensify the many social problems of the city. In 1910, a survey of the living standards of these people found that 78 per cent of the average family's income accounted for food and rent alone, which left very little for clothing, fuel or other necessities. A mere five thousand tenement houses had to accommodate over a third of the population. Four-fifths of these tenements were one-roomed dwellings, some declared unfit for human habitation. By 1914, the city's death rate was the fifth highest in the world. The chief causes of mortality of the time were: the exposure of ill-clad children to bad weather; improper and insufficient feeding of infants; overcrowding; prevalence of tuberculosis; lack of nourishment; and an excess of drink.

Mrs. Gogan's daughter Mollser who is suffering from consumption, Fluther with his drink problem, Rosie Redmond who lives in a single room and had to scrape a living as a prostitute, and Bessie Burgess who lives in a tiny attic room with its 'unmistakable air of poverty bordering on destitution' [*Act IV, line 6*] are more typical as examples of the prevalent conditions of the tenements at the time.

THE HISTORICAL CONTEXT

The outbreak of war

Acts I and II of *The Plough and the Stars* are set in late 1915; Acts III and IV, during the Rising of Easter Week, 1916—a crucial period in terms of modern Irish history. The outbreak of war between the United Kingdom and Germany in 1914 was to be felt in Ireland in a number of different ways. It meant the Home Rule Act was suspended for the duration of the war. The war quickly stimulated the Irish economy so that there was soon plenty of money in circulation. By April 1916, there were 150,000 Irishmen on active service abroad—motivated to some degree by the fact that Belgium was Roman Catholic. In Act I, Bessie Burgess tells us that her only son is away fighting in the 'threnches' *[590]*; and in Act II, Bessie (though she is a Protestant) wonders 'how they can call themselves Catholics, when they won't lift a finger to help poor little Catholic Belgium' *[279]*. By and large, though, many Irish nationalists such as John Redmond were content to wait for peace to bring Home Rule to Ireland while the country enjoyed the profits of war in the meantime. It is worth bearing in mind that the notion of an insurrection at this time was by no means a popular one. It was Eoin MacNeill, chief of staff of the Irish Volunteers, who wrote in February 1916 that:

> . . . *of this I am certain, that the only possible basis for a successful revolutionary action is deep and widespread popular discontent. We have only to look about us in the streets to realise that no such condition exists in Ireland.*

Pearse and Connolly

But even so, there were those more militant nationalists who, though in a minority, wanted complete separation from Great Britain and regarded the war as an ideal opportunity to forward this end. They had resolved that before the war ended, the independence of Ireland should be asserted in arms. The most characteristic representative of this viewpoint was Patrick Pearse, who makes an appearance in the play as 'The Figure in the Window' of Act II. Pearse believed that a 'blood-sacrifice' such as was being witnessed in Europe must be made in Ireland if we were to redeem 'the failure of the last generation'.

James Connolly, leader of the Irish Citizen Army (which was formed in 1913 by Jim Larkin to protect striking workers), was also resolved on insurrection. In January of 1916, Connolly was persuaded by Pearse to accept a scheme of combined action. Jack Clitheroe, we are told, is a Commandant in the Irish Citizen Army, which is why he becomes involved in the Rising.

O'Casey had been a particularly active member of the Citizen Army and fully supported its commitment to socialist ideas, but he could not accept its association with the more militant members of the Council of the Irish Volunteers. In Act I, through the character of The Covey, O'Casey makes clear his own viewpoint on this matter. Referring to the Citizen Army flag, the Plough and the Stars, The Covey tells Clitheroe that it 'was never meant for politics' *[649]*, and that 'It's flag that should only be used when we're buildin' th' barricades to fight for a Workers' Republic!' *[652]*.

The Rising condemned

This condemnation of the Easter Rising lies at the heart of *The Plough and the Stars*. It is there in the The Covey's words but also in the way O'Casey presents the sentiments of Pearse, and, to a lesser extent, Connolly in Act II. The high-sounding rhetoric of the Figure in the Window is set against the drunken buffoonery of those in the bar. It is there in the way he portrays Capt. Brennan (a chicken butcher) and Clitheroe as no more than selfish, vain men. And it is there, ultimately, in the terrible price the Rising is seen to inflict on innocent civilians such as Nora Clitheroe, her stillborn child, and Bessie Burgess. The historian F.S.L. Lyons tells us that 'For the citizens in general the Rising began as a spectacle, became an inconvenience and ended in tragedy,' and this is precisely the manner in which O'Casey presents the insurrection to us, with all the pomp and ceremony of Act I and Act II, the heart-rending agony of Act III and the insane tragedy of the final act.

Those who took part in the Rising had to face up to the unpleasant fact that they were acting very much on their own initiative and not by popular decree. Though the famous proclamation Pearse read aloud in front of the burning GPO summoned all Irish people to rally behind them, the insurrectionists were regarded with disdain, and public opinion was utterly hostile to them. The Rising had virtually paralysed the city, food soon grew scarce and privations among the poor were especially severe. *The Freeman's Journal*, the most widely-read paper in the country, declared on 5 May that, 'The insurrection was no more an insurrection against the connection with the Empire, than it was an armed assault against the will and decision of the Irish nation itself constitutionally ascertained through its proper representatives.'

Thus, while condemning the men of 1916 and cheering on the government troops, many of the spectators took quick advantage of the situation and began wrecking, looting and burning shops and stores. Act III of *The Plough and the Stars* documents this paradoxical situation. Capt. Brennan and Clitheroe enter carrying the mortally wounded Langon. Brennan is furious with Clitheroe for not shooting at the street mobs. Clitheroe maintains that he could not shoot fellow 'Irish men an' women', *[527]*. 'Irish be damned!' Brennan savagely retorts, 'Attackin' an' mobbin' th' men that are riskin' their lives for them. If these slum lice gather at our heels again, plug one o' them, or I'll shock them with a shot or two meself!' *[529]*

It is to Clitheroe's credit that he sees the contradiction inherent in shooting these people whom he is supposed to be defending against the tyranny of British rule. But O'Casey still manages to bring home quite clearly the point that the Easter Rising of 1916 happened against the will of the people, and in many cases it left them worse off than before. The ill-gotten gains of looting, which people like Fluther, Uncle Peter, the Covey, Bessie and Mrs. Gogan enjoyed, hardly compensated for the long-term damage inflicted upon the city.

Futility versus Nobility

The initial hostility to the insurgent leaders was not to last. Between 3 May and 12 May, fifteen of them, including all the signatories of the proclamation, were executed. This, more than anything else, served to sway Irish opinion towards the insurgents. This was why *The Plough and the Stars*, written ten years after the Rising, was greeted with riots. To be seen to condemn the men of 1916, to suggest that they were misguided and foolhardy, and that the people on the streets behaved as they had, was to commit a sacrilege.

O'Casey steadfastly refused to romanticise the Rising, to view it as Yeats did in his poem *1916*, when he described the events as a 'terrible beauty'. While Yeats saw nobility, O'Casey saw only futility. It is true that O'Casey sees no merit in the obvious element of self-sacrifice displayed by the men of 1916. The Irish Citizen Army combined with the Irish Volunteers would not have exceeded 1,600, and such numbers against the might of the British army suggests that military victory in itself was never expected. Connolly is reported to have told a friend that 'we are going to be slaughtered'. O'Casey does not deal directly with this aspect of the Rising, but it is implied that such a conscious decision to die for one's country was, in this instance, inappropriate, to say the least. The appalling social conditions as described above had still to be tackled.

A LOVE STORY

The Plough and the Stars is clearly a political play, but it is also important to remember that it is a play about individuals. The history and the politics are treated as a backdrop, though they eventually do intrude on the lives of these individuals. Essentially the play is a love story with Nora and Jack Clitheroe as the chief protagonists. Because so much happens during the course of the play, and because many of the other characters are larger than life and far more engaging, this is a fact that is often overlooked. Put very simply, it is the story of Nora's love for her husband, Jack Clitheroe, and how the Rising separates them, eventually causing Jack's death, the loss of their first child and Nora's sanity. Everything else is incidental to this central story, for it is around Jack and Nora that O'Casey patterns and paints the life of the tenements and the events of the Rising.

And it is from this relationship that we derive the central metaphor of the play. As Nora and Jack are torn apart so, too, are the city and its people. As Jack turns on Nora in Act III and throws her to the ground, Capt. Brennan threatens to turn on the 'slum lice' of the tenements. And as Nora's sanity slips away and one senseless death follows another in rapid succession, the insanity of those who took it upon themselves to bring about the Rising becomes all too obvious. It is no accident that O'Casey puts such words of wisdom into the mouth of the innocent child, Mollser, in Act I, *[963]*, 'Is there anybody goin', Mrs. Clitheroe, with a thither o' sense?'

1880 30 March, born at 85 Upper Dorset Street, Dublin. Baptised
      John Casey at St Mary's Church, Church of Ireland.
      Parnell elected chairman of Irish Parliamentary party and
      later tried for conspiracy.
1886 O'Casey's father dies at the age of forty-nine.
1891 Death of Parnell.
1893 Foundation of Gaelic League.
1895 O'Casey acts the role of Father Dolan, the patriotic priest
      in Dion Boucicault's *The Shaughran* at the old Mechanics
      Theatre in Abbey Street—the same theatre would be rebuilt
      as the Abbey Theatre nine years later.
1898 First issue of Connolly's '*Workers' Republic*'.
1900 O'Casey teaches Sunday School at St Barnabas Church,
      North Wall, Dublin.
1902 Irish Literary Theatre becomes the Irish National Theatre
      Society.
1903 O'Casey works as a labourer on the Great Northern Railway
      of Ireland.
1904 The Abbey Theatre opened.
1906 O'Casey learns Irish, joins the Drumcondra Branch of the
      Gaelic League and gaelicised his name to Seán O'Cathasaigh.
1907 O'Casey joins the St Laurence O'Toole club and writes his
      first stories and articles for the club's *Manuscript Journal*,
      which was read at meetings.
      O'Casey's *Sound the Loud Trumpet* published in *The Peasant*
      and *Irish Ireland*.
1909 Irish Transport and General Workers' Union formed; James
      Larkin becomes general secretary.
1910 O'Casey is founder member and secretary of St Laurence
      O'Toole Pipers' Band.
1911 O'Casey joins ITGWU.
1913 O'Casey is secretary of the Women and Childrens' Relief
      fund during the general strike and lockout; also secretary of
      Wolfe Tone Memorial Committee.
      Irish Citizen Army is founded.
      Irish Volunteers is founded.
1914 O'Casey's brother Tom dies, aged forty-four.
      O'Casey becomes secretary of Irish Citizen Army.
      Britain declares war on Germany.
      Supreme council of IRB decides on an insurrection before
      the end of the war.

1915   Pearse's oration at the funeral of O'Donovan Rossa.

1916   Easter Rising begins in Dublin 24 April. O'Casey plays no part in Rising.

Pearse orders surrender 29 April.

Leaders of Rising are executed (3-12 May).

1918   O'Casey's sister, Isabella dies, aged fifty-two.

End of war in Europe.

1919   O'Casey's booklet, *The Story of the Irish Citizen Army*, is published.

Dáil Éireann adopts provisional constitutions and declaration of independence.

Anglo-Irish war lasting until 1921.

1920   Abbey Theatre rejects O'Casey's first two scripts.

1921   Anglo-Irish treaty.

1922   The Abbey rejects two more of O'Casey's scripts.

Treaty approved by Dáil Éireann.

The Civil War begins.

1923   O'Casey's *The Shadow of a Gunman* opens at the Abbey (12 April).

O'Casey's next play, *Cathleen Listens In*, opens at the Abbey (1 October).

End of the Civil War.

1924   *Juno and the Peacock* opens at the Abbey (3 March).

O'Casey's *Nannies Night Out* opens at the Abbey.

1926   *The Plough and the Stars* opens at the Abbey (8 February).

Riots at the Abbey over *The Plough and the Stars*.

1927   O'Casey marries Eileen Reynolds-Carey in Chelsea.

1964   O'Casey dies of a second heart attack in Torbay, England.

PART TWO

General Summary

After O'Casey strips away the illusions and self-deceptions of which men are guilty what remains is the sense of life in its harsh actuality and the need for acceptance and sympathy despite, or rather because of, the betrayals and human limitations the play has enacted.

(Michael W. Kaufman, 1972)

THE OVERALL STORY

The play is divided into four separate acts and charts the effects of the 1916 Easter Rising on a group of tenement folk, particularly Nora and her husband, Jack Clitheroe. Sharing the Clitheroes' two-roomed dwelling are Peter Flynn (Nora's uncle) and The Young Covey (Jack's cousin). We are also introduced to Bessie Burgess (a street fruit-vendor) who lives in a tiny attic room at the top of the building; the charwoman Mrs. Gogan and her sickly daughter Mollser who live in another part of the same building; and, finally, Fluther Good the carpenter. The other characters in the play, such as Langon or Brennan, Rosie Redmond or the Figure in the Window, though significant to the play as a whole, are known to us on a much less intimate basis.

Act I
  The play opens in Jack and Nora Clitheroe's home, a Dublin tenement, in November 1915. Britain is at war with Germany and the streets of Dublin are tense with expectation. Revolution is in the air, with the Citizen Army and the Irish Volunteers marching in the streets and their leaders making rousing speeches against Great Britain. There is tension between Bessie Burgess and Nora, whom Bessie regards as something of a snob. There is tension, though somewhat comical, between the pompous Uncle Peter and The Covey, who takes great delight in needling the old man. There is also a palpable tension between Nora and her husband Jack. Clitheroe has left the Citizen Army for Nora's sake, and, it is suggested, because he has not been promoted to Commandant. It is clear, however, that Clitheroe resents the fact that Brennan, an old flame of Nora's, has been 'made a Captain' *[Act I, 638]*. Clitheroe subsequently learns that Nora has suppressed news of his own promotion. In a fury, he abandons her to rejoin the ranks of the Citizen Army.

10

Act II

In Act II we move to a public house. Outside, a large figure is delivering a speech calling on Irish people to join ranks against the forces of the Crown and to strike out for her long-awaited independence. But the only fighting we witness is the petty squabbling of those in the pub. A slagging match between Bessie Burgess and Mrs. Gogan becomes a fist fight and The Covey is evicted by the Publican as Fluther challenges him to a fist fight for insulting a prostitute's honour. But for all of these high jinks and farcical goings on, the chilling words of the Figure in the Window leave little doubt that blood will be shed. This is reinforced by the pledges made by Capt. Brennan, Lieut. Langon and Clitheroe respectively as Act II comes to an end: 'Imprisonment for th' Independence of Ireland!', 'Wounds for th' Independence of Ireland!', 'Death for th' Independence of Ireland' *[667-670]*.

Act III

Act III takes place on the street outside of the tenement. Five months have passed. It is now Easter Week 1916, and the Rising has just begun. The various characters come and go. Amid the confusion of exploding guns and burning buildings, they indulge themselves in a looting spree. But most important of all, Clitheroe is confronted by a bewildered Nora who pleads with him to put down his arms and come home with her. Clitheroe, after a moment's hesitation, chooses instead to help carry his wounded comrade to safety. By the end of Act III, the battle on the streets has intensified and the task of finding a doctor for Nora, who has gone into labour prematurely, falls to Bessie Burgess.

Act IV

Act IV takes place in Bessie's attic room some days later. As the Rising draws to an end, Fluther, The Covey and Uncle Peter play cards beside a coffin containing the bodies of Mollser and Nora's dead infant. Bessie has been nursing Nora who has now lost all sense of reality. We learn that Clitheroe has been killed in action. But Bessie is to be the final casualty in the play. In an attempt to move Nora from the window, Bessie is mistaken for a sniper and shot in the back. The night sky in the background 'flares into a fuller and deeper red' *[674]* as two English soldiers drink tea and sing 'Keep the home fires burning' over Bessie's body.

STRUCTURE

Like most full-length plays, *The Plough* is composed of a number of minor stories, or 'plots'. A plot is basically a particular story within the play and involves one or more of the characters. The way in which these plots are interweaved is what is known as the play's structure. Because there is such a large number of distinctive characters, and because they are set against such a great upheaval as the Easter Rising, the structure of the play is quite complex. It is possible, however, to break the play down into six essential plots. In order to have a clear overview of the play, it is worth noting each of these plots, their importance to the play as a whole and how they are developed.

Six Basic Plots

1. The Rising

It is important to remember that the catalyst for all of the plots is that of the 1916 Easter Rising. It is the most important plot in terms of moving the action of the play forward. Without the Rising, there would be no conflict between Jack and Nora Clitheroe, no killings or looting, and very few of the heated arguments between The Covey and Fluther or Bessie and Mrs. Gogan would take place. The Rising is presented to us before, during, and after it takes place in order to demonstrate the way in which it passed through the city and shook the lives of one and all like an horrendous earthquake. Because we learn about the events of the Rising primarily through various reports made by each of the characters, we come closest to it in Act III as Clitheroe, Brennan and Langon come on stage. But the purpose of the Rising, from the point of view of those who led it, is, of course, articulated by The Figure in the Window of Act III.

2. Nora and Jack

Put quite simply, we have Nora who has no interest in the Rising and wishes only to improve the quality of her life and her marriage. On the other hand, there is Clitheroe with his eye on the honour and glory of what he would regard as the great cause of Irish independence. Neither one set of values or expectations can accommodate the other—hence the loss of Nora's efforts to prevent her husband from risking his life, the loss of her sanity, her child, her husband and her dreams. Bearing in mind that, in Act III, Clitheroe tells Nora that 'I wish to God I'd never left you' [550], it is also the story of the painful lesson Clitheroe learns, though only after it is too late to act on this knowledge.

3. Nora and Bessie

The relationship between Bessie and Nora undergoes a substantial change in the course of the play. It is clear from Act I that there is no love lost between Bessie and Nora. Nora's haughty, patronising

12

manner, the way in which, as Bessie puts it, she speaks 'proud things, an' lookin' like a mighty one in th' congregation o' th' people' [Act I, 564], rankles with Bessie. So does Nora's having a new lock fitted to her door, and her 'checkin' th' children playin' on th' stairs . . .' [Act I, 548]. Nora, on the other hand, has an intense fear of Bessie. So much so, that she warns Jack in Act I that 'Some day or another, when I'm here be meself, she'll come in an' do somethin' desperate' [596]. This same enmity emerges in Act III as Nora returns from her night's vigil between the barricades. Though Nora is plainly distraught, Bessie shows no signs of sympathy for her as she roars abuse down from her window. But as Clitheroe abandons Nora in Act III and leaves her on the ground, Bessie swallows her pride and runs to help. The plot has an ironic twist, however, as Bessie, whom Nora feared would one day do her harm, now carries her in out of harm's way, risks her own life in fetching a doctor, nurses her night and day, and is finally shot as she pushes Nora away from the window.

4. Fluther and Uncle Peter

Though the characters of Uncle Peter and Fluther bear little resemblance to each other, their story in relation to the Rising is one and the same. They both represent a brand of patriotism which involves a great deal of hot air but little or no action. In Act I, Fluther, in defending those taking part in the political demonstration, declares to The Covey that 'We're all Irishmen' [312], as if the distinction is of crucial importance to him. And in Act III, Fluther loses the run of himself as the words of the Figure in the Window cause him to wax lyrical about dying for Ireland [103-112]. Uncle Peter joins Fluther in a similar chorus and both men see themselves as glorious heroes of the coming revolution. By Act III, it is plain that both men want next to nothing to do with anything that might endanger their precious lives, with the possible exception of looting a few unguarded shops. By Act IV we find both men huddled together under the wing of Bessie Burgess. Admittedly Fluther surprises us by helping Mrs. Gogan to arrange things with the undertaker for Mollser's funeral, but this is not done in the name of patriotism; rather it is a measure of Fluther's generous and human character.

5. The Covey

The Covey's story holds little in the way of surprises or contradictions. From the outset he is against the Rising and spends most of his time trying to convince people that workers throughout the world should be uniting against their common enemy—that of the slave-driving Capitalist class. The irony of The Covey's story is that nobody seems to accept that there might be at least a smidgeon of sense in what he is saying. This becomes clear when, in Act IV, he tells Fluther that, given the appalling social conditions they are forced to live in, Mollser's death was inevitable: 'Sure she never got any care. How could she get it, an' th' mother out day an' night lookin' for work, an' her consumptive husband leavin' her with a baby to be born before he died!' *[64-67]*.

6. Mrs. Gogan and Mollser

In many respects, Mrs. Gogan and Mollser are hardly affected by the Rising which is precisely why their story is of significance. Mollser is already suffering from consumption when we first see her at the end of Act I. By the time she is helped back into the tenement by Bessie in Act III *[305]*, she has deteriorated even further. The sight of her coffin in Act IV hardly comes as a surprise. So high was the mortality rate of young children in the tenements, that very few families did not bury at least one child (see 'Social Context' in Introduction). Mrs. Gogan, having perhaps resigned herself to Mollser's death long since, is, as Fluther puts it, 'in her element now' *[306]*. This may seem cruel and somewhat heartless of Fluther, but his words are confirmed by Mrs. Gogan's behaviour and the tragedy of a society that allows the death of young children to become commonplace is all the more poignant for this. Mollser's death is a tragedy within the tragedy of those killed and maimed during the Rising.

ACT I

Brief Outline

The setting

The Clitheroes' home—which consists of a front and back room—in a run-down tenement building. The Covey and Uncle Peter also live here. It is November 1915.

Characters

Principal characters introduced: *Jack Clitheroe,* a twenty-four year old bricklayer and Commandant in the Irish Citizen Army and his twenty-two year old wife *Nora; Peter Flynn* who is Nora's uncle and *The Young Covey* who is Clitheroe's cousin; *Fluther Good, Bessie Burgess, Mrs. Gogan* and her daughter *Mollser. Capt. Brennan* is the only character we meet in Act I who does not live in the same tenement building as the others.

The action

It is a seemingly normal day in the Clitheroe household. Fluther fixes a new lock to the door while Mrs. Gogan gossips about Nora, and Uncle Peter struggles to get into his Forester's costume. The Covey arrives home from work early because there is to be a massive political rally later that evening. Nora arrives to find Peter chasing after The Covey because he had been making fun of him. Peace restored, Bessie Burgess steps into the room and threatens Nora for telling the children on the stairs to be quiet and complaining about Bessie's nightly hymn-singing. Clitheroe arrives and, with Fluther's help, has Bessie thrown out. After tea, Nora and Clitheroe are left alone for a short while before Capt. Brennan arrives. Clitheroe learns that he has been promoted to Commandant in the Citizen Army, but also that Nora has been hiding this news from him. In a temper, Clitheroe leaves for the meeting as Nora pleads with him to stay.

Detailed Summary

The Clitheroe Household [2-38]

O'Casey gives his usual detailed description of the set, which is a two-roomed tenement rented by the Clitheroes. Our attention is drawn to the overall state of disrepair the room is in '. . . struggling for its life against the assaults of time, and the more savage assaults of the tenants' *[3]*. But O'Casey also points out that the main room is 'furnished in a way that suggests an attempt towards a finer expression of domestic life' *[13]*, which is an obvious reference to Nora's housekeeping. The richly coloured cloth between front and back rooms, we are told, is 'dark purple, decorated with a design in reddish-purple and cream' *[8]*. The classical pictures of 'The Sleeping Venus' and Millet's 'The Angelus' and 'The Gleaners', the candlesticks 'of dark carved wood' all combine to give us our first impression of Nora's character; her determination to keep up the appearance of the home despite its being no more than a tenement flat in the heart of Dublin's slums.

Fluther and Uncle Peter [39-75]

There are lengthy descriptions of Fluther Good, who is repairing a door lock, and Uncle Peter, who is airing a shirt by the fire. Both men are described very much in humorous terms—Fluther with his bent nose, his bald head and scrubby red moustache, his faded jerry hat and black bow; Uncle Peter, in his stockinged feet, wearing only a singlet and white whipcord knee-breeches, his face 'shaped like a lozenge', and his 'straggling wiry beard of a dirty-white and lemon hue' *[66]*.

Mrs. Gogan and the parcel [76-108]

Mrs. Gogan enters carrying a parcel for Nora which she has taken from the postman. Her entrance embarrasses the half-clad Uncle Peter who marches into the other room in a fury. She is described, among other things, as being 'fidgety and nervous, terribly talkative' *[90]*, and this is confirmed within minutes of her arrival. So great is Mrs. Gogan's curiosity that she has to open Nora's parcel, finding it to be an elaborately decorated hat.

Mrs. Gogan discusses the Clitheroes [109-221]

The first conversation between Fluther Good and Mrs. Gogan is really an overly-long description of Nora and Jack Clitheroe in their absence. Mrs. Gogan strongly suspects that their marriage is deteriorating. Nora, Mrs. Gogan believes, is trying too hard to please her husband. She tells Fluther how Nora Clitheroe is getting above herself with her polite ways, her stylish clothes and her contempt for the tenement way of life. Jack Clitheroe, we are told, has left the Citizen Army, much to Nora's relief, because he wasn't promoted to Captain. Mrs. Gogan describes how he used to stand in the doorway showing off his 'Sam Browne belt' *[195]*. Fluther tells Mrs. Gogan that Uncle Peter is preparing himself for a political gathering later that night in Parnell Square *[170]*. This same meeting takes place outside of the pub in Act II.

A comical interlude [222-284]

Soon after this, Fluther gives a small cough. Noticing this, Mrs. Gogan tells him of a woman who had a tickle in her throat one night which led to her death the following morning. At first Fluther dismisses this, but then imagines the cough is getting worse. This comical interlude comes to a climax as Mrs. Gogan holds Uncle Peter's shroud-like shirt up to Fluther to see how he might look in it.

The Covey and Fluther argue [285-381]

It is because of this political meeting that The Covey returns home early from work. The argument between Fluther and The Covey on the subject of religion that follows is in fact the result of a misunderstanding. The Covey points out that those attending the meeting will have to 'renew their political baptismal vows to be faithful in seculo seculorum' [301], meaning they will reassert their promise of allegiance to the Republican cause. Fluther, misunderstanding The Covey, tells him to keep religion out of things. But religion has not been mentioned. The Covey is trying to make the point that, since men are made up of the same assortment of 'mollycewels and atoms' [318], the concept of a nationality is meaningless. This is all above Fluther's head and by now he is becoming impatient with The Covey's insults. The argument is reduced to a name-calling verbal battle, The Covey calling Fluther an '. . . oul', ignorant savage [371], and Fluther returning the compliment by describing The Covey as '. . . a word-weavin' little ignorant yahoo of a red flag Socialist!' [380].

The Covey and Uncle Peter argue [382-524]

Though Mrs. Gogan's embarrassment at the sight of the naked Venus over the fireplace is a trivial, minor incident, it does underline how different she is from Nora, who would regard such a picture as a 'tasteful' thing to have in her flat. It is also evident that neither Fluther nor Uncle Peter appreciate the picture. After Mrs. Gogan exits, Uncle Peter and The Covey launch into a petty argument which is brought to a sudden halt by Nora's entrance. They are both given a good ticking off as a mother might warn two children to behave themselves. It is significant that Nora's last word on the subject is that she does not want the house in an uproar when Clitheroe comes home from work [521-524].

Enter Bessie Burgess [524-566]

It is just after Nora has paid Fluther for fixing the lock—and after Fluther has assured her that he is off the drink—that Bessie Burgess makes her first entrance. Bessie has a number of complaints to make against Nora, such as why she has been stopping the children from playing on the stairs and why she has been complaining about Bessie's hymn-singing. Although we are not told so, there is every possibility that Bessie has been drinking, which might account for her extreme behaviour. This short scene manages to shift the lighthearted quality of Act I to a more serious mood. We are told that Bessie looks 'scornfully and viciously at Nora' *[543]*. Bessie actually forces her way into the room and physically attacks Nora. It is Fluther who manages to restrain Bessie.

Enter Jack Clitheroe [567-704]

Clitheroe enters and, realising what has happened, warns Bessie not to be interfering with Nora. Fluther gently eases Bessie out as she declares that her son, who is fighting in Flanders, would be quick to support her. At this point, Nora delivers an important line in the play—in view of Bessie's later behaviour—when she tells Clitheroe that she believes 'Some day or another, when I'm here be meself, she'll come in an' do somethin' desperate' *[596]*. There follows another two arguments. In the first, The Covey tells Clitheroe that the Citizen Army flag (The Plough and the Stars) should not be used for national politics but for 'buildin' th' barricades to fight for a Workers' Republic' *[653]*. And there is a second and final argument between The Covey and Uncle Peter which culminates in both men leaving for the political demonstration.

Nora and Clitheroe are left alone [705-920]

The tension between Nora and Clitheroe quickly becomes evident. Nora is anxious to discourage Clitheroe from attending the political demonstration later that evening, but Clitheroe's restlessness would suggest that he would like to go, if only to see Capt. Brennan, '. . . swankin' it at th' head of the Citizen Army . . .' *[640]*. Clitheroe tells Nora that he gave the army up for her, while Nora maintains he did so only because he wasn't made a Captain. The tension eases somewhat as Nora tries on the hat he bought her for her birthday and he sings to her. But this mood is soon reversed as Capt. Brennan arrives and informs Clitheroe that he has been promoted after all and that Nora had known about this all along. Clitheroe has been ordered to 'take command of the eighth battalion of the I.C.A.' *[851]* during the night's demonstration. In pleading with Clitheroe to ignore his orders, Nora warns him that 'Your vanity'll be th' ruin of you an' me yet . . .' *[892]*, little realising just how accurate her prediction will prove to be. Clitheroe dons his Sam Browne belt and his army hat and leaves Nora weeping.

Enter Mollser Gogan and Bessie [921-964]

The pathetic figure of Mollser comes into the room. We are told that consumption has 'shrivelled her up' *[922]*, so much so that she could be mistaken for a ten-year-old child and not the fifteen-year-old she really is. Mollser has been left alone by her mother and has

come to Nora because she is frightened that she might 'die sometime when I'm be meself . . .' *[928]*. Mollser and Nora sit in silence
as the Dublin Fusiliers are heard singing 'It's a long way to
Tipperary' on their way to the front in France. Bessie appears at the
door once more and predicts that those who ignore their duty (i.e.
refuse to fight against the Germans) and plot instead against the
government forces will come to a bad end. The final words are left
to Mollser who wonders 'Is there anybody goin', Mrs. Clitheroe,
with a titther o' sense?' *[963]*.

Commentary

Themes touched on in Act I

There is nothing seemingly unusual about Act I as the curtain
rises and we find Fluther Good fixing a lock on the door and Mrs.
Gogan entering with a parcel for Nora Clitheroe. It is a simple,
domestic scene with no hint of the catastrophic events that will unfold in later acts.

Very little actually happens in this act, as O'Casey uses it, more or
less, to introduce us to the principal characters and their relationships to one another. He also uses it to 'fill us in' on some of the
political events then in progress, and which, in subsequent acts, will
become important parts of the play as a whole.

The most important event in Act I is the revelation that Jack
Clitheroe has been promoted to the rank of Commandant in the
Irish Citizen Army, and that his wife, Nora, has being concealing
this information from him. The argument between Nora and Jack is
in fact the climax of Act I. Up to this point, and Jack's departure,
the act consists of a series of harmless arguments on different topics:
in a somewhat confused argument, Fluther and The Covey argue over
Nationalism, socialism and religion; The Covey needles Uncle Peter
who flies into a rage twice as a result; Nora and Bessie Burgess come
to blows; Clitheroe abandons Nora and returns to the Citizen
Army. Each of these arguments, however, tells us something about
each of the characters. And although Act I presents us with such an
array of colourful, clownish characters as well as a serious love story,
there are a number of key topics touched upon for the first time.

We are first made aware of the political background to the play
when Fluther reads from a handbill the details of a patriotic march
to be held that evening in the city. This leads into Mrs. Gogan's
description of Clitheroe's involvement in the Citizen Army—an army
of volunteers originally intended to protect the striking workers.

The Covey objects to the Citizen Army involving itself in nationalistic politics. A staunch socialist, The Covey believes the workers
should fight for the rights of workers and not involve themselves in

the fight for Independence against Britain. This is why The Covey talks of there being no such thing as an 'Irishman, or an Englishman, or a German or a Turk; we're all only human bein's' *[314]*.

Peter is dressing himself up in the costume of the Foresters. Unlike the Citizen Army, the Foresters harken back to a more romantic vision of Ireland and did little more than to march to Wolfe Tone's grave each year to honour his memory (Peter refers to this in Act II, line 82).

Although these points of view are treated lightheartedly, they were serious issues at the time, and as the play progresses, the implications of each becomes more clear. It is the Citizen Army which draws Clitheroe away from Nora. There is an element of the Foresters' romanticism in the rhetoric used by the Figure in the Window of Act II. For all his faults, there could well be something in The Covey's objections to nationalism and its questionable value to humanity in general.

Bessie's appearance draws our attention to the larger, perhaps more important, war being fought against Germany. While the consumptive Mollser's 'I do be terrible afraid I'll die sometime when I'm be meself' *[928]* reminds us of the real poverty and deprivation those in the tenements suffered.

Serious and comical characters

One of the more obvious features of Act I is the huge contrast between the light, humorous first half, leading up to Peter and The Covey's exit, and the dark tension of second half. The distinction between the two is very clear if we compare any of the arguments between the other characters with the concluding argument between Nora and Clitheroe. While we can laugh at the absurdity of Peter chasing The Covey about the room with a sword, or Fluther's describing The Covey as a 'word-weavin' little ignorant yahoo of a red flag Socialist!' *[380]*, our reaction to Clitheroe telling Nora that 'You deserve to be hurt . . .' *[901]* would certainly not be that of laughter.

We must keep in mind then that *The Plough* works on both a serious plane as well as a comical one, and that it does this by presenting us with comical characters like Fluther, Peter, Mrs. Gogan and The Covey on the one hand, and Bessie, Mollser, Nora and Clitheroe on the other (though Bessie is seen in a more amusing light in Acts II and III). This distinction between comedy and more serious moments is obvious in Act I, but becomes less distinct as we move into Act II.

Ironic conclusion

The conclusion to Act I in particular is steeped in irony. There is irony in Mollser's words as she enters after the fracas between Nora

20

and Clitheroe has ended and Clitheroe has left. Mollser tells Nora how envious she is of her and her strength in keeping 'a home together for a man' *[932]* little knowing that the Clitheroe household is already beginning to fall apart despite Nora's best efforts. The new lock on Nora's door is hardly fortification enough against the turmoil of the world outside. The Fusiliers are heard singing as they pass by on their way to the front in France. Bessie, like a messenger of doom, echoes Nora's earlier prophecy for those who remain behind: '. . . they'll be scattered abroad, like th' dust in th' darkness!' *[958]*. Yet again there is a painful irony in Bessie's words in that, unbeknownst to her, she also will meet this darkness. As Bessie lies dying in Act IV, she cries to Nora, 'Jesus Christ, me sight's goin'! It's all dark, dark!' *[610]*.

Important Lines in Act I

The following notable lines, and those listed for Acts II, III and IV, relate to all-important aspects of studying the play. They indicate one or more of the following: features of a character's personality, relationships between characters, an underlying theme, important ironies, and various examples of the kinds of language used by different characters.

Nora:
(to Peter and The Covey) Are yous always goin' to be tearin' down th' little bit of respectability that a body's thryin' to build up? *[485]*

'I'm not goin' to have th' quiet of his (i.e. Clitheroe's) evenin' tossed about in an' everlastin' uproar . . .' *[522]*

(to Fluther) You're a whole man. *[529]*

(to The Covey) Willie, is that th' place for your dungarees? *[606]*

(to The Covey) Willie, brush your clothes before you go. *[661]*

(to Clitheroe) . . . you gave it up (i.e. the Citizen Army)— because you got th' sulks when they didn't make a Captain of you. It wasn't for my sake, Jack. *[724]*

(to Clitheroe) Your vanity'll be th' ruin of you an' me yet . . . *[892]*

The Covey:
(to Clitheroe) Because it's a Labour flag, an' was never meant for politics. . . . What does th' design of th' field plough, bearin' on it th' stars of th' heavenly plough, mean, if it's not Communism? It's a flag that should only be used when we're buildin' th' barricades to fight for a workers' Republic! *[649-654]*

(referring to Peter) Looking like th' illegitimate son of an illegitimate child of a corporal in th' Mexican army! *[687]*

Fluther:
(Fluther's repeated use of the word 'derogatory' and the phrase 'vice versa' throughout the play should be noted)

. . . no more dhrink for Fluther. *[177]*

(referring to Mrs. Gogan) You can't sneeze but that oul' one wants to know th' why an' th' wherefore. . . . *[281]*

I think we ought to have as great a regard for religion as we can, so as to keep it out of as many things as possible. *[304]*

(referring to The Covey) . . . thryin' to juggle Fluther's mind with complicated cunundhrums of mollycewels an' atoms. *[323]*

Mrs. Gogan:
(Note the fact that, during this act, Mrs. Gogan spends most of her time gossiping about the other main characters in the play.)

It always gives meself a kind of threspassin' joy to feel meself movin' along in a mournin' coach, an' me thinkin' that, maybe, th' next funeral'll be me own, an' glad, in a quiet way, that this is somebody else's. *[249]*

Clitheroe:
To-night is th' first chance that Brennan has got of showing himself off since they made a Captain of him—why, God only knows. *[637]*

(to Nora) You were always at me to give up th' Citizen Army, an' I gave it up; surely that ought to satisfy you. *[721]*

Uncle Peter:
(Peter's alliterative language and the amount of contradictions he makes should be noted in particular.)

She makes these collars as stiff with starch as a shinin' band o' solid steel! *[336]*

(to Nora) Would you like to be called a lemon-whiskered oul' swine? *[499]*

Bessie Burgess:
(referring to Nora) Why is she always thryin' to speak proud things an' lookin' like a mighty one in th' congregation o' th' people! *[564]*

An' ladyship an' all, as some of them may be, they'll be scattered abroad, like th' dust in th' darkness! *[957]*

Mollser:
Is there anybody goin', Mrs. Clitheroe, with a titther o' sense? *[963]*

ACT II

Brief Outline

While the meeting is going on outside, the occupants of the pub rail and shout abuse at one another. Two 'camps' are formed with Bessie Burgess and The Covey—both objecting to the sentiments of the Figure in the Window, on one side—and Mrs. Gogan, Uncle Peter and Fluther on the other. As the Figure in the Window calls on all Irishmen to take up arms, so Bessie and Mrs. Gogan come to blows, and Uncle Peter is left holding the baby. Fluther then challenges The Covey, who has insulted the prostitute, Rosie Redmond. Before The Covey can retaliate, he is evicted by the Barman, and Fluther takes Rosie into the snug. Finally, Capt. Brennan, Lieut. Langon and Clitheroe enter carrying the Citizen Army flag and the Irish Tricolour. Each swears an oath of their allegiance to the cause of Irish Independence above all else.

The setting

A public house somewhere in the city centre. The political demonstration referred to a number of times in Act I is about to conclude outside. In effect, the setting extends onto the street since we are able to see the person delivering the speech to the crowd as a large figure through the window at the back of the bar, and we can hear the crowds as they react to his words. The bar also has a snug which is a separate small compartment for customers wishing to drink in privacy. Snugs were once very common features of Irish pubs.

The characters

There are a number of new characters introduced in Act II: *The Barman* who has very little to do other than to serve drinks and break up fights—of which there are no shortage in this act; *Rosie Redmond*, a prostitute intent on picking up a customer but having difficulty because all the menfolk seem to be more interested in the demonstration; *The Voice of the Man*, the figure we see through the window of the bar who delivers the rousing speech to the gathered crowds; *Lieut. Langon* who is wearing an Irish Volunteers' uniform. At this time, part of the Volunteers had joined forces with the Citizen Army (ref. 'The Historical Context' page 4).

The action

Act II, like Act I, is made up of a series of arguments, only this time they are more heated and the characters, such as Bessie and Mrs. Gogan, do come to blows; The Covey and Fluther come within a hair's breadth of a fist fight. The action, then, is fast and aggressive.

Detailed Summary

Rosie Redmond [1-49]

Act II begins with Rosie, a prostitute, in conversation with the Barman. She paints a picture of the marching crowds in the streets which immediately undermines whatever romantic or heroic image such a spectacle might conjure up: 'You'd think they were th' glorious company of th' saints, an' th' noble army of martyrs thrampin' through th' streets of paradise' [34]. Rosie's one concern is to get a customer so she can pay her rent. Unfortunately for Rosie, however, the men are 'thinking of higher things than a girl's garthers' [37].

The Figure in the Window's first speech [54-63]

The first speech from the Man silhouetted in the window is the first of his many calls to arms throughout Act II. His 'Bloodshed is a cleansing and sanctifying thing' [58] is one of the most significant lines in the play as it is precisely this sentiment which O'Casey is objecting to. But, coming directly after Rosie has given an account of her financial problems (rent, food, laundry and clothes), this grandiose speech is made to sound somewhat hollow. Throughout the act there is always this contrast.

Enter Fluther and Peter [64-121]

Fluther and Peter dash into the pub brimming 'with the fullness of emotional passion' [174], having heard the emotive words of the orator. Fluther and Peter, as they consume numerous drinks, immediately launch into lengthy rhetorical speeches of their own. Their words may not be as impressive nor as inspiring as those of the Figure in the Window, but what we are seeing is the hypnotic effect of the orator's words. Both Peter and Fluther imagine themselves as potential warriors in some romantic battle. Fluther calls out that 'th' spirit of a man is pulsin' to be out fightin' for th' truth' [81]. Peter tells him, 'Every nerve in me body was quiverin' to do somethin' desperate!' [101].

The Figure in the Window's second speech [122-136]

Yet again the Speaker calls for men to be ready and happy to sacrifice themselves on the battle field. The great irony here is between the Speaker's words and the actions of Fluther and Peter. As the Speaker compares the spilling of blood to that of red wine, as in the sacrament of the mass, our two heroes 'gulp' down their own drinks before returning to the meeting. It is this juxtaposition of events inside a pub, with the supposedly glorious speech of the Figure in the Window, which constantly undermines the Speaker's eloquent words.

Enter The Covey [137-207]

The Covey now enters and Rosie thinks she might at last have a customer. But The Covey is even more belligerent than in Act I. Unlike Fluther and Peter, his response to the Speaker's words is a negative one. 'Freedom,' he asks Rosie, 'What's th' use o' freedom, if it's not economic freedom?' *[165].* And though there may be something in what The Covey says, his saying this to Rosie—who couldn't care less—along with his other Marxist pronouncement that 'There's only one freedom for th' workin' man: conthrol o' th' means o' production, rates of exchange, an' th' means of disthribution' *[178],* causes him to sound just as comical and outrageous as Peter and Fluther. A little slow on the uptake at first, The Covey finally realises what Rosie is up to. He runs from the pub.

Enter Mrs. Gogan [208-269]

Fluther and Peter enter once again, accompanied by Mrs. Gogan who is 'carrying a baby in her arms' *[214].* Yet again we see an example of Mrs. Gogan's fascination with death as she tells Fluther how Peter's ostrich plumes bring to mind the somewhat comical image of each Forester 'hangin' at th' end of a rope, your eyes bulgin' an' your legs twistin' an' jerkin', gaspin' an' gaspin' for breath while yous are thryin' to die for Ireland!' *[238].* Peter attempts to defend himself by pointing out that he has never missed a single pilgrimage to Wolfe Tone's grave. But Fluther is not impressed and makes a final quip at Peter by pointing out to Mrs. Gogan that 'you'd wondher whether th' man was makin' fun o' th' costume, or th' costume was makin' fun o' th' man!' *[267].*

Bessie and Mrs. Gogan quarrel [270-334]

The Covey re-enters with Bessie and they 'go over to the opposite end of the counter, and direct their gaze on the other group' *[273].* Bessie, as she made clear in Act I, objects to any form of insurrection in Ireland, as does The Covey. Bessie objects because she regards herself as a loyal subject of the Crown, The Covey because he believes the less-well-off would gain nothing—only a socialist revolution would please The Covey.

This is the starting point for the first bar-room brawl between Bessie and Mrs. Gogan, but, as happens in the next brawl, politics are quickly forgotten and it becomes personal. Bessie first argues that the Catholics of Ireland should be out defending the Belgian Catholics against the Germans. Clearly with her own son in mind, Bessie paints a picture of young soldiers at the front, their 'white bodies, shredded into torn an' bloody pieces' *[294].* It is a description pointedly in contrast with the romantic images of heroic death contemplated earlier by Peter and Fluther, and not unlike Nora's horrific description of a dead soldier in Act III. Mrs. Gogan quickly changes the subject and for the remainder of the argument Mrs. Gogan and Bessie hurl an endless stream of accusations and counter-accusations at one another.

The Figure in the Window's third speech [335-343]

The battle between the women is momentarily interrupted by the voice of the Speaker. Once again, when we place his words alongside the actions in the pub, we find an ironic contrast between the two. The Speaker tells the crowd outside that 'People in Ireland dread war because they do not know it' [338], while a war in miniature is being acted out in the pub behind him, and nothing any of the men can do will stop it. The Figure in the Window concludes this section of his speech by telling the crowd that they should welcome war. But at this point, neither Peter nor Fluther are too keen on the idea of a domestic fight between two women, not to mention a real war.

The women's fight resumes [344-468]

Fluther and Peter, who were earlier itching for a fight, now find themselves unable to countenance any such thing. Fluther tells Mrs. Gogan that on such a night, 'it's rompin' with th' feelin's of hope we ought to be, instead o' bein' vice versa!' [400], (advice Fluther conveniently forgets a few minutes later as he picks a fight with The Covey). Peter, who was earlier 'quiverin' to do somethin' desperate!' [102], now tells Bessie 'I'm terrible dawny, Mrs. Burgess, an' a fight leaves me weak for a long time afterwards . . .' [402]. The effect of such irony is once again to emphasise the mock-heroics of people like Peter and Fluther who are in love with the romantic idea of fighting for their country, but who can hardly face up to the prospect of actually becoming involved.

Fluther and The Covey quarrel [469-656]

The two women head out of the pub and onto the streets to finish their argument. Peter, who has been left holding Mrs. Gogan's baby, runs out after them. The second brawl begins when The Covey questions Fluther's idle boasts about what he has done for, and knows about, the Irish Labour Movement. Fluther does not take kindly to being questioned by a young upstart like this, especially in front of Rosie. When The Covey turns on Rosie as well, Fluther takes advantage of an opportunity to change the subject. He will now adopt yet another kind of romantic stance; he will stand up for this poor, defenceless woman whose honour is at stake. And so the man, who a few moments earlier told Mrs. Gogan this was not a fitting night to be fighting, now tells The Covey to 'put your mits up now, if there's a man's blood in you!' *[595]*. Before he has a chance to put Fluther's prowess to the test, The Covey is quickly removed from the pub by the Barman, and the second barroom brawl comes to an end. Fluther, naturally, sees no contradiction in the fact that earlier on he had been marching and cheering in the name of a United Ireland and is now boasting of how he almost killed a fellow Irishman. 'I hit a man last week,' he tells Rosie, 'an' he's fallin' yet!' *[625]*, and they go into the snug arm in arm. Rosie has finally found herself a customer.

The Figure in the Window's final speech [657-665]

These final words delivered by the Figure in the Window bring his whole speech to a crescendo as he tells the crowd that war is inevitable, and that Irishmen will never rest so long as the memory of the wrongs England has inflicted on the country—symbolised by the graves of the Fenian dead—are undone. '—they have left us our Fenian dead, and, while Ireland holds these graves, Ireland, unfree, shall never be at peace!' *[663]*.

Clitheroe, Brennan and Langon [666-698]

Clitheroe and Capt. Brennan of the Citizen Army, with Lieut. Langon of the Irish Volunteers, have entered in time to hear this speech. Langon has announced that Ireland is greater than a mother, Clitheroe that Ireland is greater than a wife (the only reference to Nora in this act). We are told the three men are 'mesmerized by the fervency of the speeches' *[643]*. It is dangerous emotion because, unlike Peter and Fluther, these armed men are willing and determined to sacrifice both themselves and others as a result of the poetry and passion of the Speaker. As a drunken Fluther comes out of the snug with Rosie singing to him, we hear the soldiers outside being ordered to march away.

Commentary

A general picture

Act II is a more general act than Act I in that there is no single person or relationship at its centre. It is meant to be a general picture of the way in which ordinary people were dragged into the false rhetoric, i.e. the poetry and passion of men such as Pearse and Connolly—represented by the Figure in the Window—of violence and the possibility of glorious heroism. The constant threat of violence in this act anticipates and prepares us for the bloody events of the next two acts. After Act II, we move back once again to Nora and how all of this is affecting her.

Three important features of Act II

Act II has three basic functions. As we would expect, it tells us a great deal more about all the main characters in the play, with the exception of Nora. Perhaps the most obvious aspect of these characters which O'Casey focuses on here is their aggressive personalities. This may have something to do with the excitement of the moment, with men marching on the streets and rabble-rousing speeches calling men to arms. But the fighting in the bar is very much an extension of the many arguments we witnessed in Act I. Here Bessie picks a fight with Mrs. Gogan instead of Nora, as she did in Act I, and the argument here develops into an actual fight. Likewise, whereas Fluther and The Covey merely agreed to disagree in Act I, here they have to be kept apart by the Barman. It is hard to escape the fact, then, that O'Casey's characters are, without exception, quite hostile. We may try to understand this as being partly a result of their environment, which forces them to behave in this way if they are to survive. But, as the following acts reveal, this hostility is not the only feature of their personalities. In fact, in the case of Bessie and Fluther in particular, there is a suggestion that the hostility is merely a 'rough exterior' concealing certain more tender attributes.

A second basic feature of Act II is the way in which the principal theme of the play (how the romantic image of the Easter Rising compared with the reality of the situation) is further developed. The romantic image is that described by the Speaker to the crowds outside the bar, of men dying heroically, of Irishmen throwing off their chains and embracing some mythical form of freedom. The reality O'Casey presents us with is one of bar-room squabbling, of prostitutes plying their trade, of men cowering behind the skirts of women. A third important aspect of Act II, which also relates to both of these functions, is the way in which language is used by each of the characters, either to hide behind or as an instrument of aggression. It is worth noting how only the women actually come to blows. (This aspect of the play is dealt with in more detail in Part 3, page 77.)

Complex structure

Act II is not as simply structured as the first act. This is because the action here, while set in a public bar, also spills out onto the street from where we hear the Speaker's words. In order to appreciate fully the irony of this act, we are meant to compare constantly the words of the Speaker outside on the street with the actions of those inside, to see how great is the contrast between this romantic visionary's words and the reality of the ordinary humble people on the street. But Act II is also complicated because of its frenetic energy. The way in which Fluther, Uncle Peter and The Covey enter

29

and exit a number of times, the fighting and brawling, the hurling of insults, all add up to a complex sequence of events. Even so, having said this, it is also true to say that Act II presents us with an even more complicated structure.

Important Lines in Act II

The Speaker:
   (All four of the Speaker's speeches are important. They are: *[54 to 61], [122 to 130], [335 to 342]* and *[657 to 665]*.)

Fluther:
   (to Peter) It's my rule never to lose me temper till it would be dethrimental to keep it. *[221]*

   (referring to Peter) . . . you'd wondher whether th' man was makin' fun o' th' costume, or th' costume was makin' fun o' th' man! *[267]*

   (to Mrs. Gogan) . . . it's rompin' with th' feelin's of hope we ought to be . . . *[400]*

   (to The Covey) Maybe, then, I done as much, an' know as much about th' Labour movement as th' chancers that are blowin' about it! *[513]*

   I hit a man last week, Rosie, an' he's fallin' yet! *[625]*

The Covey:
   What's th' use o' freedom, if it's not economic freedom? *[165]*

   (to Rosie) Look here, comrade, I'll leave here tomorrow night for you a copy of Jenersky's *Thesis on the Origin, Development, an' Consolidation of the Evolutionary Idea of the Proletariat.* *[181]*

   (referring to Peter) When I think of all th' problems in front o' th' workers, it makes me sick to be lookin' at oul' codgers goin' about dhressed up like green-accoutred figures gone asthray out of a toyshop! *[316]*

   There's only one war worth havin': th' war for th' economic emancipation of th' proletariat. *[334]*

   (to Rosie) It'll be a long time before Th' Covey takes any insthructions or reprimandin' from a prostitute! *[549]*

Bessie:

I can't for th' life o' me undherstand how they can call them-selves Catholics, when they won't lift a finger to help poor little Catholic Belgium. *[279]*

Mrs. Gogan:

(referring to Bessie) I'm not goin' to keep an unresistin' silence, an' her scattherin' her festherin' words in me face, stirrin' up every dhrop of decency in a respectable female . . .*[410]*

Clitheroe:

Ireland is greater than a wife. *[652]*

Death for th' Independence of Ireland! *[670]*

Langon:

Wounds for th' Independence of Ireland! *[668]*

ACT III

Brief outline

The setting

It is Easter week, nearly six months later, and the Rising has begun. The action takes place in the street outside the tenement building. But even from here, it is possible to see how much better off the Clitheroes are than their neighbours in the same building. O'Casey draws our attention to the front parlour windows which are hung with rich casement cloth, and we are told this is the Clitheroes' parlour. The other windows, by contrast, are 'grimy, and are draped with fluttering and soiled fragments of lace curtains' *[12]*.

The action

We see how each of the characters responds to the Rising. In the case of Nora, the effects are devastating. She has spent the night searching for Clitheroe among the barricades and gunfire, and is now at her wit's end. When Clitheroe does make a brief appearance, Nora is convinced he has deserted the Citizen Army, but Clitheroe cannot bring himself to abandon his wounded comrade. While it is true that the other characters see the Rising as a chance to loot and plunder the surrounding shops, we also see how Fluther and Bessie are ready to risk their own lives to help Nora. It is Fluther who brings Nora back from the barricades and Bessie who runs to fetch a doctor when Nora goes into labour.

Detailed Summary

Mollser [1-44]

Outside the Clitheroes' tenement home, Mrs. Gogan tries to comfort Mollser who is now in the last stages of consumption. Mollser talks 'weakly and wearily' of having a 'horrible sinkin' feelin'. Here, our attention is drawn once more to the poverty of the tenements in which children were lucky to survive to adulthood. But we are also invited to bear in mind that, to the men fighting in Rising, those starving on the streets and dying in the tenements were but a minor consideration, with very little romance attached to their cause. The Covey, as we have seen, is the only man in the play who comes near to suggesting that the fight should be for the less-well-off.

Mrs Gogan tells all [45-130]

After this relatively low key opening, things begin to hot-up as the pace speeds up. There is an air of child-like excitement rather than the oppression one might expect in such circumstances. As in Act I, it is Mrs. Gogan who gives us the details of what has happened to date. Mrs. Gogan can hardly contain her morbid imagination as she dwells first on the possibility of Clitheroe showing up 'covered with bandages, splashed all over with th' red of his own blood' *[51]*, and then Fluther 'dhressed in th' habit of Saint Francis' *[118]*. Nora has been out all night searching for Clitheroe, and Fluther has gone in search of Nora. Peter and The Covey run on, 'breathless and excited' with an account of the fight so far. There is a reference to Pearse's reading of the Proclamation outside the GPO and how the gunboat '*Helga*' is shelling Liberty Hall.

Fluther brings Nora home [131-158]

With the entrance of Fluther, 'half-leading, half carrying' Nora, the mood becomes more sombre. This is a long, slow passage, and the most direct attack on the romantic image of the Rising. Through Nora's suffering we see the reality of war. Nora tells of how futile her search has been and of how she was accused of being cowardly by those at the barricades. Jack Clitheroe, Nora tells us, 'is to be butchered as a sacrifice to th' dead!' *[157]*, the 'dead' being the same 'Fenian dead' referred to by the Speaker in his final speech of Act II. The word 'butchered' is also in stark contrast to the Speaker's religious image of blood as wine warming the 'old heart of the earth' *[124, Act II]*. Nora continues in this vein, pointing out how 'no woman gives a son or a husband to be killed' *[181]*, calling to mind that Bessie, as we learned in Act I, is a mother reluctantly separated from her son, and also reminding us of the 'Wives' and 'Mothers' summarily dismissed by Clitheroe, Brennan and Langon at the end of Act I. O'Casey draws our attention to the fact that the mothers and wives are normally the unwilling victims, the silent martyrs of mens' war games.

Bessie Burgess [159-169]

Bessie interrupts Nora by shouting down insults from her window and singing 'Rule Britannia'. Bessie seems unaware of Nora's mental state at this point as she accuses her of encouraging Clitheroe to join in with those who would stab 'in th' back th' men that are dyin' in th' trenches for them!' *[165]*. Bessie also seems to be unaware of the fact that Nora never wanted Clitheroe to take part in the fighting.

Nora describes a dead rebel [170-237]

It is here we come to Nora's description of a dead rebel. 'His face was jammed again th' stones, an' his arm was twisted round his back' *[212]*. Nora tells how the other rebels were frightened to look at the dead body. It is difficult to reconcile this image of an unsightly death at the barricades with the heroic deaths of the 'Fenian dead' referred to by the Speaker in Act II. Yet again, O'Casey emphasises the huge gulf between such romantic images of war and the reality.

The looting begins [238-515]

Again the pace changes as Nora is led indoors by Mrs. Gogan and the men begin a game of 'tossers'. For the first time, we see just how humane Bessie is under her gruff exterior as she secretly hands Mollser a cup of milk (note that it is Bessie who helps Mollser back into the house). Within minutes, however, Bessie returns on stage, loaded down with goods she has just looted from the bombed-out and burning shops. We need to keep in mind here that what we are getting is a view of the Rising from below, as it were. Rather than seeing the 'glorious' fighting, we are witnessing the opposite, less than complimentary, side of the coin. This is what the Rising meant to these people, a chance to get their hands on some of the riches normally beyond even their wildest dreams. The effect is comical, with a great deal of slap-stick, especially during the fight between Bessie and Mrs. Gogan for possession of a pram. What we have in effect is a replay of the match between the same two women in Act II. Only here, they reach a compromise, realising, no doubt, that time is of the essence. The comedy continues as Uncle Peter tries hopelessly to drum up enough courage to join the looters, and a woman from Rathmines begs for someone to help her home. The Covey returns with a ten-stone sack of flour and a side of ham on his back, soon followed by Bessie and Mrs. Gogan, their pram also laden down with looted goods.

Enter Clitheroe, Brennan and Langon [516-674]

A rifle volley brings this comic interlude to a sudden end. Brennan enters carrying the wounded Langon and followed by Clitheroe. Clitheroe is telling an angry Brennan he could not shoot the looters because 'they're Irish men and women' [527], to which Brennan responds with some of the most telling lines in the play. Referring to the Irish people who chased after and objected to the rebels, Brennan says: 'Irish be damned! Attackin' an' mobbin' th' men that are riskin' their lives for them. If these slum lice gather at our heels again, plug one o' them . . .' [529]. Langon is badly wounded and they need to get him to an ambulance in a hurry. During the following moments, he punctuates the scene with cries of pain.

Nora runs from the house to Clitheroe. He is now faced with a choice: must he desert his wounded friend, Langon, or stay with his pregnant wife who desperately needs him? The choice is impossible—either way, Clitheroe will lose out. What makes his final decision, to abandon Nora, so appalling is that he does so only after he learns of Nora's efforts to find him at the barricades. O'Casey actually tells us that Clitheroe fears 'her action would give him future shame' [613]. In the midst of such chaos with his friend dying by his side and his wife on the verge of madness, Clitheroe is still concerned about his reputation. When Brennan suggests that Clitheroe is frightened of Nora, the result is a foregone conclusion; Clitheroe will not allow the heroic image he has of himself to be trodden on like this. Nora is sacrificed to save his image. Clitheroe is not acting out of any genuinely-felt loyalty to his wounded comrade. He is acting now, as ever, out of self-interest. Once again, the picture O'Casey gives us of the men fighting the Rising is not a handsome one.

Bessie comes to Nora's aid [674-680]

It is now Bessie's turn to play the Good Samaritan as she, against all our expectations, runs to help Nora who has been left by Clitheroe in a state of collapse on the ground. The irony of this particular moment brings us back to Act I, when Bessie first threatened Nora, [596, Act I]. Here we find the situation is the exact opposite; it is Clitheroe who has done 'somethin' desperate' and Bessie who has come to Nora's aid.

Fluther returns [680-741]

Within minutes of this episode, the brazen Bessie is back again, gripping the drunken, noisy Fluther by the collar and pulling him in off the street, telling him that 'I'll thrim your thricks o' dhrunken dancin' for you' [715]. Now that Clitheroe's treatment of Nora has induced premature labour, and Mollser has taken a turn for the worse, Bessie finds herself the only person willing to brave the bullets to fetch a doctor. Bessie's courage and determination is now seen to be on par with Nora's. It is left to us to guess, without too much difficulty, as to why neither Peter nor The Covey will search out a doctor for Nora. Clearly Fluther is too drunk. Pulling her shawl over her head 'as if it were a shield', Bessie prays for God's protection and moves off into the bullet-strewn streets in search of a doctor who might be willing to come to the house.

Commentary

Treatment of The Rising

In terms of the overall play, Act II brings us closest to the actual fighting on the streets. The progression is logical; the previous two acts have prepared us for this sudden explosion of violence. We have had petty bickering, family disputes, violent language, fist fights, an orator calling men to arms. It follows, then, that all of this should come to a head in this way. But, despite all of this chaos, O'Casey manages to keep a firm grip of the play's scathing attack on the consequences of the Rising. Although the civilians are, for the most part, still treated as clowns and humorous eccentrics, the men in uniform (i.e. Clitheroe and Brennan) show a distinct lack of humanity. Brennan tells Clitheroe he should not have shot over the heads of looters in the streets. Clitheroe, now realising he should never have got himself into this mess, loses his temper when he hears that Nora may have sullied his reputation by searching for him in the streets. At no point do we see the soldiers as heroes, only as frightened men, unwilling to admit to their fear. To make such an admission would be to uncover the romantic sham behind all they are doing.

The price of romance

Act III introduces the first real, unromantic images of the Rising. For this reason it can be regarded as the act which most directly questions the motives and reasoning behind the Rising. We said in the Introduction that *The Plough* is basically a love story, Nora's story, set during the time of the Easter Rising. It is this act which brings these two aspects together. The result is Clitheroe's impossible decision—loyalty to his wife or to his comrades—mid-way through this act. The point being made here by O'Casey is not a simple anti-war protest. In other circumstances, war might well have been justified, if, for example Irish people were about to be invaded and slaughtered by a foreign power. As The Covey—O'Casey's mouth-piece—points out: 'If they were fightin' for anythin' worth while, I wouldn' mind' *[194]*. Clitheroe's conflict lies at the heart of the play. He has been led on by the romance and glory of it all, but reality has caught up on him. There is always a price to pay and Clitheroe's will be his family and his own life.

Everything reversed

Another noteworthy aspect of this act is the way in which O'Casey constantly balances comedy with tragedy. In and around Nora's tragedy, there is no shortage of tom-foolery—very much along the same lines as the previous two acts. Bessie and Mrs. Gogan have yet another brilliant argument, this time over a pram. The Covey continues to poke fun at Peter. A drunken Fluther rolls on at the close of the act with no less than a gallon jar of whiskey, and on his head he wears 'a woman's vivid blue hat with gold lacing'. While Nora screams out in pain, Fluther sings 'Fluther's a jolly good fella!' *[687]*, his only worry being that some whiskey might spill from the jar. As Nora comes closer to insanity, so the actions of those around her become more absurd. Everything is turned on its head as Fluther, the great patriot of Act II, now cries out that 'Th' whole city can topple home to hell!' *[696]*. The men who are supposed to be fighting for Ireland now regard the Irish people as 'slum lice'. The women now become the heroes as Bessie faces into the bullets and Clitheroe retreats with his comrades. Everything is reversed in Act III because, finally, the truth of the situation is emerging, and it is this which allows O'Casey to place comedy alongside tragedy.

Important Lines in Act III

Nora:
They said th' women must learn to be brave an' cease to be cowardly . . . *[153]*

He (Clitheroe) is to be butchered as a sacrifice to th' dead! *[157]*

. . . there's no woman gives a son or a husband to be killed—if they say it, they're lyin', lyin', against God, Nature, an' against themselves! *[181]*

(referring to the dead rebel) . . . every twist of his body was a cry against th' terrible thing that had happened to him. *[213]*

I don't know what I'd have done, only for Fluther. I'd have been lyin' in th' streets, only for him. . . . *[232]*

Clitheroe:
. . . Nora, I wish to God I'd never left you. *[550]*

They'll say now that I sent you out th' way I'd have an excuse to bring you home. . . . Are you goin' to turn all th' risks I'm takin' into a laugh? *[622]*

Fluther:
Th' whole city can topple home to hell, for Fluther! *[696]*

The Covey:
An' then out comes General Pearse an' his staff, an', standin' in th' middle o' th' street, he reads th' Proclamation. *[93]*

If they were fightin' for anything worth while, I wouldn't mind. *[194]*

(referring to Peter) Y'oul' hypocrite, if everyone was blind you'd steal a cross off an ass's back! *[471]*

Mrs. Gogan:
(referring to Mollser) She's never any other way but faintin'! *[506]*

Bessie Burgess:
A lot o' vipers, that's what th' Irish people is! *[250]*

ACT IV

Brief Outline

The setting

We are in one of Bessie's two small attic rooms. It is semi-dark, with just two candles at either end of Mollser's coffin for light. A few days have elapsed since the events of the previous act and now the Rising is drawing to an end. O'Casey draws our attention to the desolate state of Bessie's home, its tiny size, the 'torn and soiled' walls *[7]*, a worn-out dresser and a single armchair, the 'Tattered remains of cheap lace curtains' *[16]* draping the window. Because there are still snipers about, it is dangerous to step outside, and in the night time sky 'the glare of the burning buildings in the town can be seen' *[26]*.

The action

The action of this act is similar to that of the first act, in that very little actually happens until right at the end. The play has come full circle, beginning in the relative security of the Clitheroes' home, moving on to the excitement of Acts II and III, and once more settling down in the final act to a series of similar arguments between the same characters in a single room. A great deal of Act IV is taken up with telling us what has happened within the last few days, as in the first act a good deal of time was taken up with informing us about the various characters. So, as the men play cards, we learn of Mollser's death and Nora's still-born child. We are told that Nora is not at all well psychologically, though it is not certain whether this is the result of the drugs she has taken or the traumatic experience she has just undergone. Bessie, we are told, has been nursing Nora day and night, and Fluther has proved his worth by daring the bullets and shells to arrange for Mollser's funeral. Brennan gives an account of Clitheroe's death beneath the flames of the Plough and the Stars. The only death we witness in the entire play is Bessie's as she is shot in the mistaken belief that she is a sniper. Over her dead body the English soldiers, who have also lost a number of friends in the fighting, sing 'Keep the home fires burning', with the optimistic refrain 'There's a silver lining/Through the dark cloud shining'.

Detailed Summary

The situation to date [1-90]

As Peter, The Covey and Fluther play cards at the foot of Mollser's coffin, we learn that Nora's still-born child is also in the coffin and that Nora herself is completely bewildered. The Covey points out that she may 'never be th' same' *[73]*. All of this information is given to us in snippets between petty arguments and disputes over the men's card game, with the red light of the burning city in the background, the calls of 'Red Cross Ambulance' coming from the streets, and Nora's occasional moans coming from the adjacent room. The men try to speak in whispers and worry that they may be discovered by the English soldiers and taken away. The Covey is quick to point out that Mollser's death was the result of poverty and neglect—unavoidable neglect, as her mother (Mrs. Gogan) was forever trying to find work, and poverty because her father had died of consumption at an early age *[64]*. In a sense, O'Casey is making sure that we do not lose sight of the fact that poverty was the real 'enemy within' at the time of the Rising, and the battle around the characters at this point would do nothing to alleviate the situation. If anything, it would cause a further deterioration, wrecking homes and leaving more fatherless families to be fed. The Covey is also the first to point out that Bessie has stayed by Nora's side 'for th' past three nights, hand runnin' *[81]*. And Fluther, who certainly showed some sympathy for Bessie in Act I as he helped her out of Nora's rooms, and who calmed Clitheroe down, now admits he always had a good opinion of Bessie. It would be difficult to doubt the truth of Fluther's words here; this gives us yet another clue to the attractive side of Fluther's character.

Enter Bessie and Capt. Brennan [91-166]

Bessie enters, barely able to stand or keep her own eyes open. She tells the others how Nora's mind seems to be lost in 'madly minglin' memories of th' past. . . .' *[115]*, at which point Brennan enters with the news of Clitheroe's death shrouded in the flames of the Plough and the Stars. Brennan's description of Clitheroe's death brings us back to the rhetorical language of the Figure in the Window of Act II. It is difficult to believe he is actually telling the truth. We are told Clitheroe's last whisper was: '. . . Tell Nora to be brave; that I'm ready to meet my God, an' that I'm proud to die for Ireland . . .' *[161]*. There is also something suspicious about Brennan's plea that 'I had to leave him to save meself . . . (He shows some holes in his coat) Look at th' way a machine-gun tore at me coat, as I belted out o' th' buildin'. . . *[151]*. Brennan is now in civilian clothing. The bullet holes in his civilian jacket would suggest that he was shot at later on, and not as he ran from the burning building. He would have needed to carry his civilian clothes with him during the fight—during Act II, he was carrying no such parcel. Ironically, Clitheroe's death was more than likely the result of being deserted by the very person who accused him of being a 'renegade' *[Act III, 633]*. Bessie is the first to accuse Brennan: 'you left him!

You twined his Rosary beads round his fingers, an' then you run like a hare to get out o' danger!' *[157]*. But Brennan refuses to face up to the reality of what has happened. He tells Bessie of the General's response: '"Clitheroe's end was a gleam of glory. . . ." Mrs. Clitheroe's grief will be a joy when she realises that she had a hero for a husband' *[164]*. The sight of Nora as she enters soon changes Brennan's mind, and exposes his words as meaningless rhetoric. He makes no further references to Clitheroe and it soon becomes apparent that the only reason he is here is because he needs a place to lie low *[272]* and not out of consideration for his comrade's widow, as he would have us believe.

Enter Nora [167-284]

In any case, there would be hardly any point in Brennan's telling Nora of her husband's death since she has now lost almost all sense of reality and imagines she is walking in the countryside with Clitheroe. Ironically, Nora—a victim to the romantic rhetoric of the rebel leaders—now escapes the harsh reality of what has happened by drifting mentally into this pastoral, romantic world. She hasn't lost all sense of the real world, however, and the most painful moments are when she momentarily realises what has happened, calls for her baby and accuses, probably Brennan, of murdering her husband. Nora turns for comfort to Bessie at such moments, and she cries, 'For God's sake, don't leave me, Bessie. Hold my hand, put your arms round me!' *[226]*. Bessie sings a hymn to quiet Nora, as Clitheroe had done in Act I, the words of which, promising light and happiness after the long dark night *[251]*, have a poignant irony to them since Bessie will not live to see the morning.

Enter Mrs. Gogan and Corporal Stoddart [285-385]

Mrs. Gogan follows Corporal Stoddart into the room as they come to collect Mollser's coffin. Mrs. Gogan is quick to sing Fluther's praises for having risked life and limb in getting hold of an undertaker. Mrs. Gogan cannot avoid the temptation to elaborate on Fluther's fearless brush with death, in searching out an undertaker: 'When all me own were afraid to put their noses out, you plunged like a good one through hummin' bullets, an' they knockin' fire out o' th' road, tinklin' through th' frightened windows, an' splashin' themselves to pieces on th' walls!' *[354]*. The interesting thing about this is that Fluther never cares to mention such genuinely brave deeds, while in Act II, he goes out of his way to let The Covey know of his more dubious valorous deeds. Mrs. Gogan then acknowledges Bessie's kindness to Mollser while she was alive, an instance of which we witnessed in Act III as Bessie slipped a mug of milk to the ailing child sitting outside the tenement building.

41

Bessie's wounded son [386-400]

Corporal Stoddart makes the mistake of associating Bessie with the rebels by calling her a 'Shinner'. Worn and tired as Bessie is, this is one insult she will not take lying down. Bessie launches into a blistering counter-attack, informing the unsuspecting Corporal that Bessie Burgess 'had no thruck with anything spotted be th' fingers o' th' Fenians . . .' [392]. She swears her allegiance to king and country and doesn't forget to mention her son 'in th' first contingent of the Dublin Fusiliers, an' that's on his way home carryin' a shattered arm. . . .' [397]. Bessie has clearly been suffering in silence, caring for Nora without letting on to anybody about her wounded son. Once again, we can see just how strong and unselfish Bessie is as a character. The cruel irony of her death is that it will be by a bullet from an English soldier's gun.

The final moments of comedy [401-509]

Before the men leave to spend the night under guard in a Protestant church, there is one final round of verbal comedy as Peter, in his own inimical way, warns The Covey and Fluther not to be getting at him. Peter is so angry he even tells Stoddart to mind his own business. But it is Fluther who has the final grand line in verbal wit as Sergeant Tinley complains that the rebel snipers are not fighting fair. 'Fight fair!' retorts Fluther. 'A few hundhred scrawls o' chaps with a couple o' guns an' Rosary beads, again' a hundhred thousand thrained men with horse, fut, an' artillery . . . an' he wants us to fight fair? D'ye want us to come out in our skins an' throw stones?' [484]. Now back on form, Fluther leaves the stage threatening to beat the two soldiers single-handed. It is as fitting an exit as we could expect from Fluther, undaunted and proud of himself, as well he might be.

Bessie's death [510-633]

Believing she is still in her own home, Nora re-enters and begins to set the table for Clitheroe's return. She sings the same song Clitheroe had sung to her in Act I. Bessie enters and, in trying to push Nora from the window, is shot twice in the back. Her death is neither sentimentalised nor used to completely white-wash Bessie's character. She dies cursing Nora and praying for mercy, begging Nora to help her and cursing the day she came to Nora's aid. Bessie dies an unglamorous, pitiful death, in great pain and in great fear, as Mrs. Gogan tells us, 'Her face has written on it th' shock o' sudden agony' [654].

The final irony [634-698]

Over Bessie's body, Stoddart and Tinley sing of keeping the home fires burning, while outside, the city of Dublin is engulfed in flames. The soldiers sing of returning home, oblivious to the fact that Bessie's son, also an English soldier, is now on his way home to his mother. It is the final cruel irony of the play.

Commentary

The internal struggle

While we might well describe Act IV as a dark and sombre act, especially when compared with the first three acts, it is by no means gloomy or oppressive. Just as the men played cards at the foot of Mollser's coffin, so the English soldiers, who have also lost friends in fighting, sing of keeping 'the home fires burning' with Bessie's body at their feet. This should not be interpreted as callous or disrespectful. These are no ordinary circumstances. It is part of an internal struggle by each person to remain on top of what is a tragic situation, it is part of the overall fight to survive; in the words of Dylan Thomas, a fight 'against the dying of the light'. Because O'Casey always retained implicit faith in the goodness of humanity, he chose to draw certain of his characters with a unique, undaunted spirit of their own. This internal struggle is perhaps one of the few fights they do win . . . in their own way.

Irony of final act

Because Act IV brings the events of the play to a final conclusion, there is a great deal of irony to be found in what the characters do and say. There are many contradictions, such as when characters like Bessie and Fluther behave in an unexpected way, or when we learn that Nora, so envied by Mollser, is now just as lost and destitute as the child herself was—in fact, Nora is to be taken to Mollser's bed as a final refuge after Bessie's death. In Part 4, on 'Other Important Features' of the play, there are more such examples of *dramatic irony* listed.

A final image of the Rising

On a more general level, Act IV can be viewed as a final, unglamorous image of the Rising. Husbands, wives and children are sacrificed and the city of Dublin is in ruins. But what has been achieved? The English soldiers themselves are seen as ordinary men, longing to return home to their families. Here we can see how false were the glorious descriptions of war and the promise by the Speaker in Act II that it would purge the country of all its ills.

Important Lines in Act IV

The Covey:
(referring to Mollser) Sure she never got any care. How could she get it, an' th' mother out day an' night lookin' for work, an' her consumptive husband leavin' her with a baby to be born before he died! *[64]*

(referring to Bessie) I don't know what we'd have done only for oul' Bessie: up with her (i.e. Nora) for th' past three nights, hand runnin'. *[79]*

D'ye know, comrade, that more die o' consumption than are killed in th' wars? *[316]*

Fluther:
It's damned hard lines to think of her (Nora's) dead-born kiddie lyin' there in th' arms o' poor little Mollser. *[61]*

I always knew there was never anything really derogatory wrong with poor oul' Bessie. *[82]*

(referring to his supply of whiskey) Spread it out? Keep a sup for to-morrow? How th' hell does a fella know there'll be any to-morrow? *[105]*

(referring to Mrs. Gogan) Sure, she's in her element now, woman, mixin' earth to earth, an' ashes t'ashes an' dust to dust, an' revellin' in plumes an' hearses, last days an' judgements! *[306]*

Fight fair! A few hundhred scrawls o' chaps with a couple o' guns an' Rosary beads, again' a hundhred thousand thrained men with horse, fut, an' artillery . . . an' he wants us to fight fair? D'ye want us to come out in our skins an' throw stones? *[484]*

Jasus, you an' your guns! Leave them down, an' I'd beat th' two o' yous without sweatin'! *[504]*

Capt. Brennan:
An' then, I seen The Plough an' th' Stars fallin' like a shot as th' roof crashed in, an' where I'd left poor Jack was nothin' but a leppin' spout o' flame! *[153]*

Mrs. Clitheroe's grief will be a joy when she realizes that she has had a hero for a husband. *[165]*

44

Bessie:

(to Brennan) Ay, you left him! (Clitheroe) You twined his Rosary beads round his fingers an' then you run like a hare to get out o' danger! *[57]*

(comforting Nora) . . . rememberin' that sorrow may endure for th' night, but joy cometh' in th' mornin'. . . . *[234]*

Bessie Burgess is no Shinner, an' never had no thruck with anything spotted be th' fingers o' th' Fenians . . . whose only son when to th' front in th' first contingent of the Dublin Fusiliers, an' that's on his way home carryin' a shattered arm that he got fightin' for his king an' counthry! *[392]*

(to Nora, after she has been shot) I've got this through . . . through you . . . through you, you bitch, you! *[582]*

Jesus Christ, me sight's goin'! It's all dark, dark! Nora, hold me hand! *[610]*

Mrs. Gogan:

I'll never forget what you done for me, Fluther, goin' around at th' risk of your life . . . *[351]*

(to Nora) Come on with me, dear, an' doss in poor Mollser's bed . . . *[659]*

PART 3

Analysis

CHARACTER STUDY POINTS

*Throughout the play, the frailty and humanity of
these magnificently rude mechanicals, led by Fluther
Good, Jinnie Gogan, Bessie Burgess, Peter Flynn and
The Covey, mock the holiness of war.*

(David Krause)

Approaching a Study of Character

This section is purposely titled 'Character Study Points' because it is
intended to touch on some of the most interesting and significant
aspects of the primary characters, rather than reducing them to
some imaginary, finite set of points. This involves two basic steps.

First, we must provide an account of their external features and
their immediate behavioural characteristics. This is more descriptive
than anything else; a great deal can be read into O'Casey's characters from the way they look and their mannerisms—facial features,
the way they talk, walk etc. (It is more along these lines that Pass
students should be working.)

The next step (and one which is more appropriate to the Honours
student) is more complicated because it involves forming an opinion
of the characters' behaviour, trying to judge their actions and their
words, and, perhaps most important of all, how they relate to other
people. Are they selfish, inward-looking people, or open, generous-
spirited people? There can never be simple right and wrong answers
to such questions, but it is important to be able to justify whatever
opinions you form. This, naturally, can only be done by referring to
the text.

Static or developing characters

A play may have characters who change or develop as the action
of the play progresses. An innocent character may be more wise by
the end of the play as a result of some experiences; an optimistic
character may become more pessimistic; an evil character may be
reformed etc. The interesting thing about all of the characters in
The Plough is that no one of them actually undergoes such a change.
The tragic nature of the play means that, by the close of play, things
have gone too far for those who might have learned something. This
applies to Clitheroe in particular, whose death makes it impossible
to see the folly of what he has done.

46

O'Casey's characters are too set in their ways, too distinctive to change, even when, as with Fluther who wants to give up drinking, they may wish to be better people. These are fully-rounded characters with all the foibles and nuances, the contradictions and motivations of real people. So that when Bessie's character seems to have altered by the end of Act III, the change is more apparent than real. Much the same can be said of Fluther. We are forced to change our opinions of them as we come to know them better. It would be wrong then to describe them as 'static' characters because such a term suggests that they lack depth, which clearly they do not. Mrs. Gogan, Uncle Peter and The Covey are borderline cases in this respect, since they give us very little reason to reassess our first impressions of them in the light of what happens during the play.

A note of caution

As a final note of caution, it should be pointed out that to treat 'character' in isolation is in itself an artificial exercise. It should always be borne in mind that characters and themes are in reality inextricably knotted together in the play, the one shedding light on the other and vice versa. Similarly, studying the text of a play is also artificial: it can never replace the experience of being a spectator confronted by flesh and blood actors. Artificial though it may be, however, like a false limb, it may still serve a worthwhile purpose.

Nora Clitheroe

Although Nora is the central character of the play, and events revolve about her struggle to keep her husband and home together, we nevertheless do not learn a great deal more about her as an individual as the play progresses. It is Mrs. Gogan who first tells us that Nora is worried because Clitheroe is no longer paying her much attention and that she is unhappy living in the tenements. O'Casey's description of Nora as 'a young woman of twenty-two, alert, swift, full of nervous energy, and a little anxious to get on in the world' *[Act I, 464]*, accurately sums up Nora as she is presented to us. In the first act she is indeed 'alert' and 'swift' as she orders Peter and The Covey about, preparing the tea and pays Fluther for mending the lock. But there is also that 'nervous energy' O'Casey refers to and which becomes more obvious as Act I progresses. It is there in her anxiousness to have the house in order for Clitheroe's return, in the way she tries to keep his mind off the march by flirting with him and asking him to sing for her. It is difficult to know if this 'nervous energy' is related to the fact that Nora has burnt the letter containing the news of Clitheroe's promotion and she is, naturally, concerned that she might be discovered, or if she is normally like this. There is also the possibility, and here we can only guess, that Nora knows she is pregnant and for whatever reason has not yet told her husband. This possibility raises an interesting question: would not news of Nora's pregnancy have softened Clitheroe, made him think twice about returning to the Citizen Army?

Love or an obsession?

Nora's function in the overall scheme of the play is to show just how devastating the Rising was at the basic level of human relationships. And yet, as we can see, Nora and Clitheroe's relationship has a certain fragility to it from the outset. Clitheroe is more than happy to leave Nora for the Citizen Army, and Nora is unable to match this attraction. But Nora is wise enough to see through Clitheroe and his comrades in so far as she recognises their insincerity to the cause of fighting for Ireland. In Act I she tells Clitheroe: 'That's what's movin' you: because they've made an officer of you, you'll make a glorious cause of what you're doin' *[883]*, and later, in Act III, she talks of the fear the rebels will not admit to as they ignore the body of a comrade between the barricades.

Nora's extreme emotional and psychological dependence on Clitheroe stands out in stark contrast to that of O'Casey's other women, both in *The Plough* and his earlier play, *Juno and the Paycock*. Nora's strength of character pales, for example, if we compare her to Mary Boyle in *Juno* who is the same age as Nora. Mary Boyle is involved in the Labour Movement and is an avid reader of progressive-thinking books. Like Nora, she wishes to rise above the poverty and degradation of tenement life, but she is an intelligent, strong-willed individual. Nora seems unable to contemplate life without her husband. While we would have to accept Nora's words in Act III, when she says that 'no woman gives a son or a husband to be killed' *[181]*, there is an uneasy element of fanaticism in her words. Or is 'fanaticism' the wrong word to use here? Could we not say that Nora's desperation is a measure of her love? Such open questions are what make Nora such a complex character.

The point is that her husband has made his decision and there is nothing she can do to change that. And yet she persists to such a degree that she cannot feel sympathy for Langon as he lies dying at her feet. It could be argued that this is not love but an obsession, an inability to adapt and accept what has to be, just as Bessie accepts that her only son, whom she loves dearly, is now fighting at the front. Mrs. Gogan has lost her husband, and, in the course of the play, her daughter. But she has not lost her sanity. Nora's single-minded determination to hold onto her husband at all costs would seem, ultimately, to betray a weakness of character not often found in

O'Casey's portrayal of women, and certainly not to be found in either Bessie or Mrs. Gogan.

An ambiguous character

If we look closely enough at O'Casey's description of Nora in Act I, we will find that he, too, has certain reservations about her character: 'The firm lines of her face are considerable opposed by a soft, amorous mouth and gentle eyes. When her firmness fails her, she persuades with her feminine charm' [467]. Reading between the lines, are we being told that this woman can be deceptive, that she is willing to use whatever means she can to get her own way? And what of Nora's attire, her 'tailor-made costume' and 'silver fox fur'? Like Nora's new hat, these must have 'cost more than a penny'. These are some questions Nora's character raises, outside of the fact that she is undoubtedly yet another victim of the Rising.

Bessie Burgess

Because our opinion of Bessie undergoes a radical change as events unfold, she is a somewhat more complex character than Nora. Bessie should be the outsider of the play—her loyalty is to the British Crown and her religion is Protestant. On both of these counts, Bessie is in a minority, although there was a much larger Protestant population in Dublin at the time than there now is. But Bessie is a fiercely independent woman, determined to be her own mistress, to let people know who and what she stands for. There is an honesty about Bessie which cuts right across the hypocrisy and posturing of those who, in Fluther's words, make an 'oath of fealty to th' Irish Republic' [Act I, 174]. Even in the face of mounting hostility, during Act III, Bessie continues to quote from the Authorised Version of the Bible, to sing her Protestant hymns and 'Rule Britannia', and to let it be known how much she despises those who have chosen to betray the men fighting against the Germans.

Bessie's character and appearance

Physically, Bessie has an imposing appearance. O'Casey tells us 'She is a woman of forty, vigorously built. Her face is a dogged one, hardened by toil, and a little coarsened by drink' [Act I, 539]. There is always a wealth of information in O'Casey's descriptions of his character's faces, and here is no exception. Bessie, though somewhat worn by the struggle to survive tenement life, has also been hardened by the experience. Though coarsened by drink, there is a dogged persistence about her of which we come to see an ample amount during the play. Her vigorous build is matched by her strength of character, and there is something about O'Casey's use of the word 'toil' which hints at his own admiration for this sterling woman. Bessie's appearance may not be as attractive as Nora's, yet, if we compare the two descriptions, Bessie's earthy, tough exterior speaks more of her humane personality than Nora's polished appearance.

A woman of the tenements

But Bessie is twice Nora's age and all the more wise for that. Her attack on Nora in Act I serves to emphasise just how different the two women are. While Nora wishes to insulate herself from the rest of the tenement folk, Bessie finds this inexplicable. Bessie's first speech shows us how much she takes for granted the communal nature of living in the tenements: 'Puttin' a new lock on her door . . . afraid her poor neighbours ud break through an' steal . . .' or 'checkin' th' children playin' on th' stairs . . . gettin' on th' nerves of your ladyship. . . . Complainin' about Bessie Burgess singin' her hymns at night' [545]. Looking carefully at these lines, it is possible to see just how much respect for her neighbours and their children Bessie has. (Remember how Bessie secretly slips a mug to Mollser in Act III.)

A contradiction in character

If there is a contradiction here, it is between Bessie's rough-mouthed manner and her essential humanity. This contradiction is there throughout the play, but it only becomes particularly evident later on in Act III, when Bessie comes to Nora's aid, just moments after she has been bellowing out insults at Clitheroe and Brennan. Bessie seems to be unaware of the fact that Nora objects to Clitheroe's participation in the Rising, but she is still capable of placing such a strongly-held prejudice to one side, to such an extent that she risks her life by fetching a doctor for Nora. But at no point does Bessie soften or become sentimental. Even as she fights off sleep in Act IV, she refuses to be classed as a 'Shinner', or a Sinn Fein supporter, by Corporal Stoddart. Having nursed Nora for three days and three nights, Bessie still insists that she 'never had no thruck with anything spotted be th' fingers o' th' Fenians' [393].

The implications of Bessie's character

For all of Bessie's noisy, objectionable characteristics, she demonstrates one over-riding quality, that is an ability to tolerate and forgive her neighbours, however much she might disagree with, even despise, their beliefs. In Act IV, Bessie shelters Brennan and refuses to betray him to the English soldiers when they ask how many men there are in the house. And yet Brennan is one of the men Bessie accuses in Act III of 'Turnin' bitther into sweet, an' sweet into bitther. . . .

Stabbin' in th' back th' men that are dyin' in th' threnches for them! *[164]*. Bessie's own son happens to be one of the men in the trenches. Once again, what we have is an example of Bessie's actions contradicting her harsh words. The obvious implications in Bessie's character is that a great deal of bloodshed might have been prevented if the rebels fighting on the streets of Dublin could have practised a fraction of Bessie's toleration. Bessie's unexpected death at the end of the play is one of the most moving scenes in the entire play.

Fluther Good

Second only to Bessie as a character of great humanity and goodwill is Fluther Good—his surname being an obvious clue to his character and his first name perhaps referring to his fondness for drink. At one and the same time, Fluther is a clown, a braggart, a poser, a pseudo-philosopher, quick-witted, courageous, amiable, a drunkard and many more things besides.

Fluther as a character of contradictions

Like Bessie, Fluther is a character of contradictions. On the one hand, we are not meant to take him seriously as he vows he is about to give up drink; as he imagines (with a little encouragement from Mrs. Gogan) that his cough is going to kill him; as he brags of what he has done for the Labour movement; how he'd love to die for Ireland, or how the man he hit last week is 'fallin' yet!' *[Act II, 626]*. He has some of the funniest, sharpest lines in the play including: 'I think we ought to have as great regard for religion as we can, so as to keep it out of as many things as possible' *[Act I, 304]*; his retort to Sergeant Tinley who maintains the rebels won't fight fair *[Act IV, 484]*; or his description of The Covey as 'a word-weavin' little ignorant yahoo of a red flag Socialist!' *[Act I, 380]*; or his comment on Peter's costume in Act II, 'you'd wondher whether th' man was makin' fun o' th' costume, or th' costume was makin' fun o' th' man!' *[267]*; or the following exchange with Bessie in Act III, after she has looted some shops:

Fluther. Ay, Bessie, did you hear of e'er a pub gettin' a shake up?
Bessie. (inside). I didn't hear o' none.
Fluther. Well, you're goin' to hear of one soon! *[310-314]*

His catch-phrase 'vice versa', and his fondness for the word 'derogatory' help to give a certain memorable charm to his character, as does his appearance, described with perceptible affection, by O'Casey as: 'bald, save for a few peeping tufts of reddish hair around his ears . . . his upper lip is hidden by a scrubby moustache . . . He

51

is dressed in a seedy black suit, cotton shirt with a short collar, and wears a very respectable little black bow. On his head is a faded jerry hat' *[Act I, 49]*. The formality of Fluther's suit, hat and black bow all suggest a vague attempt to look important, and a large part of the comedy derived from Fluther's character can be attributed to the fact that he takes himself so seriously.

A character of depth

Just how serious Fluther takes himself is most evident in the arguments with The Covey. Although Fluther shows a complete lack of scientific knowledge or historical knowledge of the Labour movement, Fluther takes on The Covey, refusing to be shown up by this young upstart who shows his elders no respect. He tells Rosie: 'I wasn't goin' to let meself be malignified by a chancer. . . . He got a little bit too derogatory for Fluther. . . . Be God, to think of a cur like that comin' to talk to a man like me!' *[Act II, 620]*. And it is in those last three words, 'a man like me', that Fluther lets us know, in no uncertain terms, what a proud man he is. It is true that Peter also takes himself very seriously, but, unlike Fluther, Peter shows absolutely no wit or sense of humour, which, as we have seen, Fluther has in abundance. And, of course, there is more depth to Fluther's character. While he boasts of unlikely altercations with dragoons in O'Connell Street, and bobby's batons at Labour meetings, Fluther never mentions that he has risked his life searching for Nora and done likewise in fetching an undertaker for Mollser. In Act I, Nora describes Fluther as 'a whole man' *[529]*, and in Act IV, Mrs. Gogan tells him that 'Mollser, in th' happy place she's gone to, won't forget to whisper, now an' again, th' name o' Fluther' *[359]*. Like Bessie, Fluther is meant to offer an alternative to the romantic ideals of the rebels and their heroic posturings. In place of such glorified causes O'Casey offers us a simple man like Fluther who, for all his faults and weaknesses, at least rises to the occasion and displays an instinctive humanity, a willingness to place himself at the disposal of his fellow human beings without indulging in pomp or mock-heroism.

The Covey

The Covey is 'twenty-five, tall, thin, with lines on his face that form a perpetual protest against life as he conceives it to be' *[Act I, 286]*. So O'Casey informs us, and, true to form, The Covey spends most of the play indulging in this 'perpetual protest'. The Covey regards himself as a socialist and is fond of quoting Marxist political jargon like 'There's only one freedom for th' workin' man: control o' th' means o' production, rates of exchange, an' th' means of disthribution' *[Act II, 178]*; or, in the same act, 'There's only one war worth havin': th' war for th' economic emancipation of th' proletariat' *[344]*. In other words, The Covey wants to see an end to poverty and inequality in society. He wants to see people earning proper wages and having more control over their own lives. We know that O'Casey felt this way too, but we also know that O'Casey fell foul of the Irish Labour Movement, in particular because of its militant activities. Which is probably why O'Casey chooses to make The Covey such a disagreeable character.

The Covey's self-righteous doctrine

It is not what The Covey is saying that O'Casey objects to, it is the way in which The Covey alienates himself from the others by acting as if he had the answers to all of society's ills. The Covey's counterpart can be found in *Juno and the Paycock* in a character called Jerry Devine who is also twenty-five and who is involved in the Labour Movement. O'Casey expresses a number of reservations about Jerry which could equally be applied to The Covey: 'He (Jerry Devine) is a type, now becoming very common in the Labour Movement, of a mind knowing enough to make the mass of his associates, who know less, a power, and too little to broaden that power for the benefit of all.' Like Jerry, The Covey gives the impression that he knows enough to tackle the injustices of society, but also like Jerry, he is incapable of doing anything with this knowledge. Nobody pays him any attention because they already know how unjust society is and they know how poor they are. The last thing the people of the tenements need is The Covey preaching his self-righteous doctrine.

The Covey's politics contradict his actions

The Covey treats socialism almost as a personal fight between him and the rest of society. Hence he directs his aggression at the people around him—Peter, Clitheroe, Fluther, Rosie Redmond—not realising that these are the people he is supposed to be defending. In effect, The Covey is caught up in theory, the academics of socialism, his actions show none of the humanity or warmth of character we find in Bessie or Fluther. The Covey is, then, also a character of contradiction. This contradiction is that, while he professes a humane political creed, at no time does he demonstrate any such humanity, sympathy or understanding for the people around him.

Perhaps the best example of The Covey's cold-heartedness is in his treatment of Rosie Redmond, when he tells her in Act II that, 'It'll be a long time before Th' Covey takes any insthructions or reprimandin' from a prostitute!' *[549]*. The fact that Rosie, a girl of twenty, is driven onto the streets to earn her living as a prostitute, is in itself a poor reflection of society. But The Covey shows no

53

appreciation of Rosie's appalling predicament. All he can do is adopt a high moralistic tone by publicly accusing her of prostitution. Rosie tells him that 'I have me feelin's' *[553]*, but feelings are not something The Covey seems to have much time for.

The Covey on Mollser's death

It should be pointed out, however, that The Covey does show a certain amount of sympathy in Act IV, when, speaking of Mollser, he points out that she died as a result of having no father to provide for her. Later, in the same act, he points out to Stoddart that 'more die o' consumption than are killed in th' wars? An' it's all because of th' system we're livin' undher?' *[317]*. But, as with Jerry Devine in *Juno*, such knowledge is hardly of any use to The Covey or to the likes of Mollser, unless somebody is willing to feel strongly enough to act upon it.

Mrs. Gogan

Of Mrs. Gogan, O'Casey tells us 'a fly could not come into nor go out of the house without her knowledge' *[Act I, 93]*. Later in Act I, Fluther gasps, 'You can't sneeze but that oul' one wants to know th' why an' th' wherefore. . . .' *[281]*. Mrs. Gogan knows everything, and O'Casey uses her as a character to inform the audience at the start of Acts I and III about what is happening. Her evaluation of the stresses and strains of Nora and Clitheroe's relationship proves to be perfectly accurate.

A lively, animated character

Mrs. Gogan has clearly had a difficult life, raising a young family without a husband's support at a time when there was very little help from the state for the poor. She has been forced to care for her family and earn money, and yet there is a lively, animated quality to her personality, especially when we compare it to, say, that of Peter or The Covey, both of whom spend the best part of their time complaining. In Act II, Mrs. Gogan proves to be more than capable of handling herself as she 'sends Peter tottering to the end of the shop' *[406]* in an effort to defend her good name against the formidable wrath of Bessie Burgess. In Act III, Mrs. Gogan puts up an equally impressive fight against Bessie for possession of a pram.

Death—a favourite subject

Mrs. Gogan has a morbid fascination with the subject of Death. In Act I, she convinces Fluther his cough might well be the death of him. Her description of how a 'big lump of a woman' *[227]* suddenly dropped down dead is the first of her many colourful accounts of death throughout the course of the play. She ruminates, with much relish, on how many unsuspecting people there are, feeling fit and healthy this very minute, but who are soon destined for the hearse. Death is a fact of Mrs. Gogan's life. Her husband has died of consumption, and soon her daughter will succumb to the same disease. But because she has romanticised death, she is drawn rather than repulsed by it. In Act III much to Mollser's discomfort, Mrs. Gogan imagines Clitheroe 'staggerin' in covered with bandages, splashed all over with th' red of his own blood . . . as his soul was passin' through th' dark doorway o' death into th' ways o' th' wondherin' dead. . . .' [51]. And in a similar vein, in the same act, she talks of Fluther's soul 'moored in th' place where th' wicked are at rest an' th' weary cease from throublin', [128]; while in Act IV she tells people that Mollser is now in a 'happy place' [359].

Typifying the women of the tenements

In many ways Mrs. Gogan is a neutral character in the play, having no part in the central drama of Nora and Jack's relationship, and no political axe to grind. Nor is she destined for such great acts of humanity as Bessie or Fluther. But Mrs. Gogan is a vital part of the play as a whole since she is the sole representative of the many tenement women who lived through, not just the trauma of the Rising, but the daily trauma of having to keep body and soul together. If at times she seems larger than life, almost a caricature, it is because O'Casey is intent on celebrating the great energy and dynamism of the people Mrs. Gogan typifies. It is, after all, Mrs. Gogan who takes over caring for Nora after Bessie has been shot.

Jack Clitheroe

> The latter-day Lieutenant Langons and Commandant Clitheroes are still proclaiming that 'Ireland is greater than a mother' and 'Ireland is greater than a wife' with the same blind indifference to how many lives they take, and lose, on foot of such proclamations.
>
> (Ronan Fanning)

Clitheroe is by no means the most engaging of characters in the play. He has none of their mannerisms, energy or humour. Even the language he uses is dull in comparison to Fluther's or even The Covey's. O'Casey makes certain not to give Clitheroe any obvious redeeming qualities, and makes it clear from the outset that there is very little that is outstanding about this man: 'His face has none of the strength of Nora's. It is a face in which is the desire for authority, without the power to attain it' *[Act I, 569]*. This would support the view that Clitheroe's involvement in the Citizen Army does have more to do with the pomp and glory of marching at the head of a squadron than dying for his country. Clitheroe's vanity is eventually both his and Nora's undoing, and O'Casey uses this ordinary human weakness as a means of portraying the Irish rebels in general in an unfavourable light.

Clitheroe's mood at the outset

It could be said that to generalise about the rebels' motives in this way is hardly fair. But O'Casey is more interested in drawing our attention to Nora's predicament and placing the emphasis on her, rather than on Clitheroe. The short love scene between Clitheroe and Nora in Act I introduces us to a man who is uneasy and temperamental, primarily because he would much rather be at the meeting than in Nora's company. But even in this mood, he does make an effort to ease the tension between them, going so far as to sing her a love song. It would be wrong, then, to dismiss Clitheroe as cold-hearted and uncaring. The news of his promotion does quickly tempt him back to the Citizen Army, but he is also angry at Nora for having deceived him by burning the letter, which may also account for his being so willing to leave the house.

Clitheroe as a man of action

If we are to praise Bessie and Fluther for their courage in taking to the streets during the Rising, then we must do so also for Clitheroe. He does go into action, and we see him standing by his wounded comrade Langon in Act III even though at this stage, as he admits himself, he regrets ever having left Nora. It is Clitheroe's motives that are in question, and those motives are presented by O'Casey as the motives of all those who took part in the Rising, as misguided idealism, as a desire to achieve the status of heroes. If Clitheroe has been misguided, if he is a victim of his own vanity, then his death in action is futile rather than noble, but it is difficult to condemn Clitheroe outright. Like many of the other characters, he has his failings and his weaknesses. But we ourselves are left with a choice: should we pity Clitheroe for his vulnerability or should we condemn him outright for deserting Nora? With Clitheroe, there are no easy answers.

Uncle Peter

Uncle Peter is almost more of a caricature than a fully-rounded personality. That is to say, his short temper, his childish behaviour, his exaggerated language, his absurd costume with plumed hat and swash-buckling sword, all of these elements combined cause him to seem more like a very slight comic figure in relation to the play as a whole. It is impossible to take anything about him seriously; indeed, nothing he does is all that important. In Act I he makes a lot of noise while getting dressed up for the march, then leaves. In Act II and III, he argues with and is made fun of by Fluther, The Covey and Mrs. Gogan. In the final act we have the same kind of argumentative behaviour and nothing more. Within this framework he tends to think of himself as a peaceable, religious man, while everything about what he does and says contradicts this. In Act I, just as The Covey has driven him to breaking point, Peter declares: 'I'll say nothin' . . . I'll leave you to th' day when th' all-pitiful, all-merciful, all-lovin' God'll be handin' you to th' angels to be rievin' . . . an' blastin' you!' *[420]*. Peter obviously does not realise the contradiction inherent in the idea of an 'all-merciful' God treating people in this way. A few moments later, in a rage and 'battering and pulling at the door' *[435]* in order to get at The Covey, Peter describes himself as 'a man who wouldn't say a word against his greatest enemy' *[436]*.

Even so, he does give a great deal of light relief to the play with his short temper, his extravagant costume and his determination not to be ruffled by other people's jibes. In the overall scheme of the play, he represents an older order of nationalistic romanticism. He plays his part for Ireland by marching each year to Wolfe Tone's grave in Bodenstown and putting a leaf from the grave in his prayerbook.

MINOR CHARACTERS

Rosie Redmond

I wonder how many of the rioters even noticed that the mischievous O'Casey had given Rosie the same surname as the greatest of the Parnellites!

(Hugh Leonard)

A survivor

Rosie Redmond makes one appearance in Act II and can therefore hardly be regarded as a 'character' in the proper sense. We are not given enough time to learn more about her as a personality. She does, however, give us a good picture of the difficult life she leads, having to 'make up fifty-five shillin's a week for your keep an' laundhry, an' then taxin' you a quid for your own room if you bring home a friend for th' night. . . .' *[44]*. During Act II we get a chance to see how she 'operates' by flattering potential customers such as

57

The Covey and Fluther and persuading them to buy her a drink. Though Rosie is presented as a tough, sharp-mouthed woman, she is yet another victim of the tenements, a girl of twenty having to resort to prostitution just to survive, and having to put up with the kind of ignorant abuse levelled at her by the likes of The Covey.

Though we tend to take it for granted today, the sight of a prostitute on an Irish stage was not something to which Irish audiences were accustomed then, and O'Casey was accused of slandering the purity of Irish womanhood. Rosie's song at the end of the act had in fact to be cut from the first production.

But in her brief appearance, Rosie does bear testament, yet again, to the strength of character and determination to survive, whatever the odds, of women as portrayed by O'Casey.

Capt. Brennan

A coward and a rival?

It is suggested that between Brennan and Clitheroe there is a certain rivalry. Clitheroe reminds Nora in Act I that Brennan 'was sweet on you, once. . . .' *[642]*. And there is something unsettling about the way in which Brennan '*softly whistles "The Soldiers' Song"*' *[910]*, as Nora begs Clitheroe not to go out. This callousness is all the more evident in Brennan's personality when, in Act III, he describes those who live in the tenements as 'slum lice' *[531]* and tells Clitheroe he should have shot some of them for 'attackin' an' mobbin' th' men that are riskin' their lives for them' *[529]*. Brennan is finally shown up for the coward he is when in Act IV, he admits having deserted the wounded Clitheroe (it is significant that in Act III, it is Brennan who persuades Clitheroe that they cannot desert the wounded Langon). Bessie does not mince her words when she tells him, 'Ay, you left him! You twined his Rosary beads round his fingers an' then you run like a hare to get out o' danger!' *[Act IV, 157]*. But Brennan seems to have learnt nothing as he repeats the General's words describing Clitheroe's death as 'a gleam of glory' *[165]*. The final irony to Brennan's character is that he finds himself being sheltered by the very people he described as slum lice in Act III.

Lieut. Langon and the English Soldiers

Ordinary men

The remaining military figures contribute very little in a direct way to the play as a whole. It is important, from an historical point of view, to remember that Lieut. Langon is an Irish Volunteer, unlike Clitheroe and Brennan who are in the Citizen Army. It is also interesting to ponder on whether or not Clitheroe might well have deserted if it were not for the fact that Langon needed his help.

The English soldiers are presented as ordinary young men and not terrible forces of evil as they might have been presented. In a fine ironic twist, O'Casey has Corporal Stoddart tell The Covey, 'I'm a Sowcialist moiself' *[Act IV, 320]*. If The Covey needed any evidence of his theory that 'there's no such thing as an' Irishman, or an' Englishman. . . .' *[314]*, as expounded to Fluther in Act I, then here it is handed to him on a plate.

The Speaker (Act II)

A theatrical device
The Speaker in Act II, strictly speaking, is not a 'character' at all. But he is a voice and his words are crucial to the play as a whole. As is well known by now, the Speaker's words are a combination of the actual words and sentiments of Patrick Pearse and James Connolly. The Speaker is what is known as a 'theatrical device'—he is inserted in the play for a specific dramatic purpose which has nothing to do with his own character. He is delivering a speech to a crowd, and therefore his words are all we are interested in, their effect on the others in Act II, and the way in which they are seen to motivate men like Clitheroe and Brennan. (The actual significance of the Speaker's words are dealt with in 'Themes' under the headings of 'History' and 'Politics'.)

A woman from Rathmines

A totally superfluous character who contributes little or nothing extra to the play, she is in fact hardly credible. This is hardly surprising since O'Casey only wrote her into the play when an actor in the original production refused to play Mrs. Gogan because she had misgivings about certain lines in the play.

THEMES

'The Plough and the Stars' is the one play in which O'Casey manages to bring political complexities and moral insight successfully together.
(Seamus Deane)

The major themes of *The Plough* can be arranged or categorised in many ways. It is such a broad play and covers so many different areas of human experience, most of which interrelate in one way or another, that no such list could possibly claim to be exhaustive or fully comprehensive. We could, for example, say that love is a theme, but love is the theme of just about everything that has ever been written about relationships, and much the same things apply to love in this play as they do in other works. The following list and treatment of themes by no means adds up to what the play is about. It is simply a breakdown of some of the more obvious subjects touched on to varying degrees by the author. The most striking of these are as follows.

Escape

It could be said that all people wish in one way or another to escape to a better, more comfortable, more rewarding way of life. Few people can afford the luxury of being able to say they are perfectly happy with their lot. The wish to get on, to improve the quality of one's life, whether for one's own sake or for the sake of family or relatives, is a natural desire, and may be broadly interpreted as a wish to somehow alter one's present state for the better. But just how desperate a person is to escape may vary a great deal. In one way or another, each of the characters in *The Plough* expresses this desire to escape, but none more so than Nora Clitheroe.

Nora's aspirations

It is clear that Nora wishes to escape from the tenements. In Act I, Mrs. Gogan quotes Nora as saying 'I wouldn't like to spend me last hour in one, let alone live me life in a tenement' *[136]*. In fact O'Casey tells us that Nora is 'a little anxious to get on' *[Act I, 466]*. But Nora's wish to escape the tenements is also reflected in the way she attempts to decorate the home so that it does not at least look or feel like a slum and the way in which, as Mrs. Gogan again tells us, Nora is concerned that Clitheroe, The Covey and Uncle Peter do not at least look as if they are from a slum. Nora is anxious to create an environment in which her relationship with Clitheroe will not undergo the obvious stresses and strains of sharing accommodation in such cramped conditions. Nora's is a noble aspiration. She wants a better life for herself and her family, but it is an aspiration she never realises. And though it is uncertain how permanent Nora's insanity in Act IV is, it does demonstrate how, driven to such an extreme, she escapes mentally into an idyllic world of flowers and birds.

Clitheroe's aspirations

Unlike Nora, Clitheroe never once voices criticism of the tenements. He has his sights set on the 'higher glory' of being a military hero. It is as if the ordinary domestic and mundane things of his life have no great interest for him. The irony is that, as Nora tries to create a comfortable family environment, Clitheroe displays all the hallmarks of a man who wishes to escape what he would probably regard as such a dull prospect. It is Mrs. Gogan who tells us in Act I that for Clitheroe 'The mystery of havin' a woman's a mystery no longer. . . .' *[126]*. And this may well be the reason why Clitheroe uses the Citizen Army as an excuse to escape his responsibilities as a husband.

Fluther and Uncle Peter

It is in Act II in particular that we see how readily Fluther and Uncle Peter indulge themselves in flights of fantasy in order to escape the humdrum reality of their lives. As the Speaker outside the bar paints a fantastic picture of war and battlefields, both these men convince themselves they are worthy opponents of the dreaded English invader. For a short time, both men escape the limitations of reality and convince themselves that they are ready and willing to die for the cause of Independence. But even without the rousing rhetoric of the Speaker, Uncle Peter, as a member of the Foresters, regards himself as an heir to the great martyrs of former generations who died for Ireland. This helps us to escape the fact that he is really very little more than a grumpy old man who never did anything for his country, and probably less for his fellowman. And the way in which Fluther picks on The Covey in Act II and the English soldiers in Act IV suggests that he pictures himself as a prize fist-fighter. He tries to convince The Covey in Act II that he received wounds for his country *[499]* and that he is an expert on the Labour Movement. In their own inimitable ways, and without harming anybody else, both men find a small quantity of dignity through this sort of escapism.

The Covey and socialism

The Covey is perhaps the most realistic character in the play in that he is able to recognise the folly of those participating in the Rising. He is likewise able to recognise how the tenement folk are deprived and exploited. For The Covey, the means of escape from this poverty trap for one and all is through Marxism. He sees the day when there will be a 'Workers' Republic' *[Act I, 654]*, when all people will be treated as equals. Though such a society would be ideal, it is perhaps a little too idealistic to imagine that Dublin society could be transformed overnight. But The Covey himself seems to be comforted by the simplistic notion that he could transform society tomorrow if only people would listen to him. In a sense, The Covey regards himself as a man with a message, a saviour, misunderstood and unappreciated by the masses. As with Fluther and Uncle Peter, The Covey's high opinions of himself can actually be seen as a way in which he escapes the reality of the environment in which he finds himself.

Bessie and Mrs.Gogan

Mrs. Gogan and Bessie Burgess are the only two characters who seem to have accepted their lot in life. Both women would have spent most of their lives, if not all, living in the tenements. Though their needs are great, their expectations are small. Mrs. Gogan does fantasise about death as if it were a dark, romantic stranger and in this way eases her pain and fear. Bessie is a proud woman and seems to be simply making the most of what is a very poor lot. But during the looting scenes of Act III, we see how thrilled both woman are to have good-quality clothes and shoes. The first things Bessie arrives with are a new hat and a fox fur *[288]*, and later in the act they return together with shoes 'with th' pointed toes an' th' cuban heels' *[493]*. So, the slums have not altogether dulled their imaginations or their need to believe in a better, more luxurious, lifestyle. They are all too aware of the fact that neither one can or ever will escape from the slums, but there is nothing to stop them dreaming.

Escaping from the chains of imperialism

It is the Speaker outside the bar in Act II who suggests that a rebellion will somehow transform Ireland. The leaders of the Rising believed that Ireland needed to escape from what they regarded as the claims of English imperialism. Ireland, freed from such bondage, they felt, would be a far better, more caring society. But, as history has shown, the manner in which they tried to break these chains showed lack of foresight and lack of vision. The War of Independence which followed on the 1916 Rising some years later would only increase the pain and hardship for many.

Poverty

The Clitheroe household

Simply because the play is set in the appalling Dublin slums at a time when surviving from one day to the next was in itself an enormous feat, *Poverty* must be regarded as an important theme in *The Plough*. But O'Casey does not treat this theme in a direct way. We do not, for example, hear about characters being hungry or unemployed, we do not see the huge underfed, half-clad families that were such a common feature of the slums. Though the Clitheroes obviously live in cramped conditions, they do not seem to lack any of the vital necessities. Relatively speaking, they are well dressed, we see them eating an evening meal, and the rooms have been decorated by Nora so as not to seem like the average, dank slum dwelling. This clearly has to do with the fact that there are three wage-earners and no children to be cared for. It should be stressed, however, that by today's standards, the Clitheroe household would easily be classed as 'underprivileged', and that full credit must be given to Nora's ability to make do so well with so little.

The real poverty

But when we look to Mrs. Gogan, a widow with a new-born infant and a tubercular child, and Bessie, who lives in a tiny attic described by O'Casey as having 'an unmistakable air of poverty bordering on destitution' *[Act IV, 6]* then we do get a first-hand taste of the real poverty that existed. In order to make ends meet, Mrs. Gogan works as a charwoman, which means having to constantly leave poor Mollser alone with the infant. It is The Covey who tells us in Act IV what little care Mollser ever got: 'How could she get it, an' th' mother out day an' night lookin' for work, an' her consumptive husband leavin' her with a baby to be born before he died!' *[64]*. Bessie, who is also a widow, makes what little she can from selling fruit on the streets. But Rosie Redmond, the prostitute we meet in Act II, is also yet another example of the extreme conditions under which these people had to survive. The fact that a girl of twenty is forced by circumstances to earn a living in this way is condemnation enough, but Rosie describes in detail the conditions of her life to the Barman: 'It's no joke thryin' to make up fifty-five shillin's a week for your keep an' laundhry, an' then taxin' you a quid for your own room if you bring home a friend for th' night. . . .' *[44]*.

The interesting thing about each of these women in relation to the theme of poverty, is how they have retained their self respect, and a certain strength of character despite all. When Bessie and Mrs. Gogan quarrel, it is noticable that they do so in terms of their own honourable reputations. In Act II, for example, the real subject of their argument is which woman is more respectable than the other. This is also the case as they argue over the pram in Act III. Each woman demands that she be respected. With Rosie, too, it is only when The Covey belittles her by saying 'It'll be a long time before Th' Covey takes any insthructions or reprimandin' from a prostitute!' *[549]*, that Rosie loses her temper.

Mollser's death

O'Casey does not, then, dwell on many of the details of what poverty meant to these people. It is presented as an obstacle which characters such as these three women prove themselves more than

63

capable of climbing. But O'Casey does not shy away from the painful fact that, for a great many people, the struggle was too much. Mollser's death is a tragedy almost overlooked as the events of the Rising and Nora's reactions to it begin to dominate the play more and more after Act II. In many ways, Mollser is a representative of the many thousands of children who died slow, silent deaths in the tenements. Though Mollser is not a major character in the play, her hopeless, poverty-stricken predicament is a major theme.

History

Two levels

History is meant to be an accurate account of an event or events that have happened in the past. An historical evaluation of a period will try to examine all the relevant circumstances in an objective fashion. Above all, it will try to look at the facts. Though this might seem a straightforward process, this is very rarely the case. No two people will tell a story in the same way. How people interpret history is often coloured by their own political and emotional prejudices. In *The Plough*, this works on a personal as well as a general level. We see how characters such as Fluther invent past deeds of valour and heroism. He tells Rosie in Act II how the man he hit last week is 'fallin' yet' *[626]*, and we have to question whether or not this ever happened or if perhaps Fluther is embellishing an account of a simple verbal argument. On a more general level, we have the leaders of the Rising telling people that war is glorious and heroic, 'a cleansing and sanctifying thing' *[Act II, 58]*. This is certainly more an emotional account of war than a factual one.

By questioning what was regarded as a glorious rebellion, *The Plough* is attempting to tackle history and rewrite it in a more factually accurate manner. It is in this sense that we can discuss *History* as a theme.

The Abbey Riots

The Plough and the Stars is regarded as a 'revisionist' play. In other words, it is taking a particular historical event—the Easter Rising of 1916—and offering a different perspective on what actually happened. When O'Casey first wrote the play, people regarded the Rising as a proud chapter in Irish history. Those who fought and died during the Rising were elevated to the status of martyrs and heroes without blemish. O'Casey questions this version of the Rising by implying that it was unnecessary, unpopular, undemocratic and carried out for all the wrong reasons. What happened, and what people had forgotten, was that it was only after fifteen rebels, including the signatories of the Proclamation, had been executed some weeks after the Rising, that people began to change their attitude. Almost overnight, nobody would dare speak ill of those who died 'for Ireland'. This was why *The Plough* caused such riots at the Abbey when it first opened. Hugh Hunt tells us:

> *The blood-sacrifice of Padraig Pearse, James Connolly and the other leaders had become a symbol of Ireland's age-long struggle for freedom. . . . By depicting the participants, not as heroes but as human beings subject to fears, the pomps and vanities of the flesh, and by showing the ordinary Dubliners as indifferent, or hostile, or having a glorious jamboree pillaging the shops, the play seemed to ardent patriots, especially those whose menfolk had perished in the event, to be a deliberate attempt to debunk the spirit that had inspired and uplifted those who took part.'*

The Plough was rewriting history and attacking what had become a popular myth. It was a deliberate 'debunking' of the romantic spirit that had inspired those who took part.

How history becomes myth

The Easter Rising was fuelled as much by idealistic notions of race and culture as it was from politics and economics. The cultural influences came from such movements as the Young Irelanders who encouraged the study of Irish history as a means of developing national self-consciousness. Poets such as Samuel Ferguson gave popular currency to heroic tales of ancient Ireland. More and more, this kind of thought emphasised the distinction between Ireland and England. The Gaelic Athletic Association, founded in 1884, cultivated what it regarded as traditional Irish games as opposed to 'foreign' games such as 'lawn tennis, polo and cricket'. The Gaelic League, founded in 1893 by Douglas Hyde, set about encouraging the growth of the Irish language. There were the so-called Anglo-Irish writers who tried to develop a distinctively national literature and of which W.B. Yeats was to become a part. The legendary Cuchulainn became a type of model for the Home Rulers. The image of Ireland as a 'poor old woman' or as Fluther describes her in Act II, the 'Shan Van Vok!' *[496]*, who would once more become a beautiful queen when men became as chivalrous as Cuchulainn, was soon widespread.

The reactions of Fluther and Uncle Peter to the Speaker in Act II show just how steeped in this romantic view of Irish history people were. They each talk of the past: Peter, 'Th' memory of all th' things that was done, an' all th' things that was suffered be th' people, was boomin' in me brain' *[99]*; Fluther, ' "You can die now, Fluther, for you've seen th' shadow-dhreams of th' past leppin' to life in th' bodies of livin' men. . . ." ' *[106]*. The language used by both men is purely poetic and emotional. Suddenly, to be an Irishman is to be a hero like Cuchalainn. O'Casey shows us how history can be mythologised and so distorted and used to drive impressionable men like Clitheroe and Brennan to take up arms. If we examine the words of the Figure in the Window of Act II, we will see that he, too, is speaking in the name of those who have sacrificed their lives for Ireland in former times, 'the young men of a former generation' *[659]*. In such sentiments, historical truth, difficult to come by at the best of times, becomes fudged, but becomes the force behind men's actions none the less. In Fluther's 'Shan Van Vok!' *[196]*, we can see how fact and fiction, myth and history become one. Even W.B. Yeats contributed to the myth of the Rising when, in his poem 'Easter 1916' he wrote:

> *And what if excess of love*
> *Bewildered them till they died*
> *I write it out in verse*
> *MacDonagh and MacBride*
>
> *And Connolly and Pearse*
> *Wherever green is worn,*
> *Are changed, changed utterly*
> *A terrible beauty is born.*

Yeats' poem immortalises men like Connolly and Pearse (whose words make up the bulk of the speech given by the Figure in the Window of Act II). *The Plough* attempts to underline the dangers and pitfalls of merging history with myth and half-truths. It was such a merger which helped to fuel the Rising.

Politics

Nationalism versus socialism

O'Casey was not a nationalist in the narrow sense of the word. He was proud of being Irish, and had a great love of his country. But if nationalism was to be regarded as an obsession at the expense of more immediate concerns, then it had to take a back seat.

He regarded himself, like The Covey, as a socialist first and foremost. He has The Covey tell Fluther, in Act I, that 'there's no such thing as an Irishman, or an Englishman, or a German or a Turk; we're all only human bein's' *[314]*. If people tried to concentrate on what they have in common rather than their differences, it is implied here, there might be a little less war in the world. This is one of the reasons why O'Casey objected to the Rising, which was motivated more by nationalistic ideals than any firm set of economic or political ideas. Like The Covey, he would have preferred to see people fighting for something more concrete, like decent housing and better wages, than for a form of nationalism which bordered on fanaticism, when men such as Clitheroe, Brennan and Langon at the end of Act III make vows declaring that there is nothing more precious to them than the cause of Ireland, not a mother or a wife.

What most angered O'Casey was that the Citizen Army, the formation of which he had played an active part, ever became involved in the Rising. The Citizen Army was formed to protect striking workers, not to combat the English forces. But Connolly believed that rebelling against the English would be a short-cut to forming an Irish socialist Republic. And so the Irish Citizen Army joined forces with part of the Irish Volunteers (of which Lieut. Langon is a representative in the play). This went against everything O'Casey had struggled for and it is why he has The Covey tell Clitheroe (who is a member of the Citizen Army) that 'They're bringin' nice disgrace on that banner now' [Act I, 645]—the banner being the Plough and the Stars, the flag of the Citizen Army.

Jingoism of Fluther and Peter

Through Fluther and Peter we see how fervant nationalism can become empty rhetoric or 'jingoism'. Jingoism means blustering patriotism, as demonstrated during Act II when Peter and Fluther run into the bar in an excited frenzy having heard the Speaker. They then launch into jingoistic speeches of how great it is to be Irishmen and ready to die for one's country. O'Casey makes fun of this because neither man is ever likely to handle a gun or take part in the fighting. They are using the notion of fighting for their country in order to increase their own self esteem. They have no intention of ever making a sacrifice, personal or otherwise, in the name of nationalism. Against this form of hollow nationalism, O'Casey is setting the more pressing social problems of the overcrowded tenements, the wives, widows and children who were on the point of starvation.

Politics overshadowed

In effect O'Casey is suggesting that we replace the contemporary political system with an alternative humane system, one that is more caring and grounded in reality. What this alternative is, O'Casey never actually tells us. Because O'Casey shares so much of The Covey's beliefs, we can gather that a socialist form of politics is by far the preferred system. But The Covey as a character does not offer any answers. In fact there is something of a contradiction in the fact that

The Covey spends most of his time fighting with or insulting other people. By portraying the poverty of the tenements, especially through Mollser's death, O'Casey attacks the political system which allows people to live under such conditions. In other words, a capitalist system which allows inequality and which exploits people by making them work long hours for low wages. But this is never directly confronted in the play because O'Casey focuses his attention on the Rising which overshadows any other politics in the play, as it did the Labour Movement at the time.

Political ideals versus romantic ideals

O'Casey is not decrying ideals in themselves. If we are to improve society, then we need to have ideals, often without much hope of ever achieving them in the short term. People like James Connolly were idealists; they wanted to achieve an independent socialist Ireland. But O'Casey maintains they went about this the wrong way; that they ignored the many pressing problems of poverty and hardship around them and not just in the city but in the country as a whole. Of Connolly, O'Casey wrote: 'The high creed of Irish nationalism became his daily rosary, while the higher creed of international humanity that had so long bubbled from his eloquent lips was silent for ever, and Irish labour lost a leader.' That is to say that Connolly had, up to this point, been putting all of his energy into socialism, a form of politics he believed would eventually become widespread throughout the world. However, Connolly was to become obsessed by the idea that Ireland could never become a socialist state so long as it was a part of Britain, which he regarded an an embodiment of capitalist imperialism. This was romantic because, from a purely practical point of view it was an impossibility. Fluther himself in the final act points out just how stacked the odds were against a successful rising: 'A few hundhred thousand thrained men with horse, fut, an' artillery. . . .' [Act IV, 484]. It was romantic because they saw it as a glorious war which would achieve instant results. It was romantic because it regarded 'dying for Ireland' as a far greater thing than living for the children, wives and mothers left behind. Through Clitheroe's treatment of his wife, and by making him out to be motivated, not by any loyalty to Ireland but by sheer vanity, imagining himself as a Captain in a glorious army, O'Casey suggests that ideals and romanticism in politics should never be allowed to go unchecked.

Heroism

Yet the heroes of these plays are not its soldiers, but their womenfolk who show courage of a different sort—who fight without sentiment and without conscious idealism to aid the suffering and afflicted and to protect their own.

(Grattan Freyer)

No more heroes

By revaluating the Rising in this way, O'Casey also introduces a different concept of *Heroism*. If there are heroes in *The Plough*, they are not the men with guns in their hands, nor are they the leaders of the Rising with their fine words and poetic turns of phrase. The three soldiers we do meet are seen to be self-centred and somewhat inhuman as, in Act II, they extol the virtues of an Independent Ireland over that of wives and mothers. But O'Casey does not give us new heroes. Instead he dispenses altogether with the idea of heroes and the romantic image normally associated with such a concept.

Bessie has her two feet firmly planted on the ground. She is a tough woman, fond of drinking and singing hymns that will annoy her neighbours. She professes to be a respectable, religious woman and yet is willing to loot and plunder the bombed-out shops. Bessie is by no means a perfect person. She is a mere human with all the failings that go with being human. Yet Bessie is by far the most unselfish, humane character in the play. And it is this quality of humanity O'Casey substitutes for glorified heroism. Much the same can be said of Fluther who, for all his human failings, is ready to do a good turn and stand by his friends and neighbours when called upon. As with Bessie, Fluther is not placed on a pedestal above and beyond his fellow human beings, for this would be to make a mock-hero of him. There is nothing glorious in what Bessie or Fluther do; it is natural and it is valuable without being pompous or egotistical. In the place of heroism, O'Casey gives us basic, humble humanity.

Violence

Violence as an expression of frustration

Violence is one of the more obvious themes in the play. It is there in many shapes and forms—verbal, physical and mental. But as well as looking at the actual acts of violence in the play, we must also examine the conditions which create or bring them about. In *The Plough*, violence, at whatever level, is inevitably the result of frustration, people frustrated with themselves; with the conditions of their lives, with their family and neighbours; with the people supposedly running the country.

Physical violence

There is, of course, the violence of the Rising itself, made most apparent in Act III as the wounded Langon is carried onto the stage. In Act IV, we hear the cries of English soldiers as a sniper picks them off from a roof-top hide. Corporal Stoddart reacts to this with a graphic description of what they will do when they catch the sniper: 'we'll give 'im the cold steel, we will. We'll jab the belly aht of 'im, we will!' *[346]*. There is Brennan's description of Clitheroe having been 'shot through th' arm, an' then through th' lung. . . . I could do nothin' for him—only watch his breath comin' an' goin' in quick, jerky gasps, an' a tiny sthream o' blood thricklin' out of his mouth, down over his lower lip. . . .' *[144]*. In Act III, Nora describes the body of a rebel as 'somethin' huddled up in a horrible tangled heap. . . . His face was jammed again th' stones, an' his arm was twisted round his back. . . .' *[221]*. The one killing we do see is Bessie's, and even here O'Casey refuses to glamorise the violence of her death as she sinks to the ground crying out for help as her eyesight fades. Terrified and in great pain, Bessie dies cursing Nora and praying to Jesus.

Verbal violence

We need, however, to distinguish *physical violence* from *verbal violence*. People are forever using threatening, abusive language. It has already been noted how the play moves from one set of arguments to another with the prospect of violence forever threatening to break out. In Act II, after a lengthy argument, Bessie and Mrs. Gogan do actually resort to physical violence. Likewise, Fluther and The Covey come close to blows once they run out of insults in the same act. Because people live in over-crowded conditions, virtually on top of each other, this is perhaps inevitable. But there is always a sense in which language is the only form of defence these people have. They assert their dignity in the face of such enormous odds by using strong language and a loud voice. This violent language is, therefore, not necessarily treated in a negative way, which is why Uncle Peter's ravings, or Bessie's battling threats give a more uplifting, invigorating feel to the play than such language might otherwise do. Violent language seems to be a natural form of expression and arguments are almost as quickly forgotten as they are started (ref. also 'Language', page 77).

Sinister forms of violence

Perhaps, though, it is the more sinister forms of violence that leave the strongest impression: Clitheroe's callous desertion of his pregnant wife; the premature birth of Nora's still-born child and the loss of her sanity; harmless Mollser's pathetic death of consumption; the cheers of the crowd in Act II as the Speaker welcomes bloodshed with open arms; Rosie having to scrape together fifty-five shillings a week for her keep and laundry; Bessie waiting, and suffering in silence, for her only son to return home crippled from the front. To deprive people of their dignity, to force them to scrimp and scrape for a living, can cause untold damage and must therefore be regarded as a form of violence.

Vanity

Vanity defined

Of his previous play, *Juno and the Paycock*, O'Casey once said: 'It is the tragedy of vanity, and of subservience to vanity'. The same could equally be said of *The Plough*. But the idea of vanity as an aspect of people which drives their ambitions, their egos, their need to impress others as well as themselves is quite complex. It would be wrong to dismiss vanity out of hand as a deadly sin. But a proper balance does have to be struck. Without a certain amount of vanity, self-respect is endangered; with too much vanity, a person can become selfish and narcissistic.

Natural vanity

Nora is clearly a woman with a significant amount of vanity. The most obvious sign of this is in the way she dresses. On her first entrance, in Act I, she is wearing 'a tailor-made costume, and wears around her neck a silver fox fur' *[471]*. These are the clothes of a woman who wants to impress people. In Nora's case, it is likely that Clitheroe, more so than anybody else, is the person she is most trying to impress. This vanity extends to her concern that the home be kept looking well. She talks to Peter and The Covey of 'thryin' to keep up a little bit of appearance' *[Act I, 489]*. There is no reason why we should fault Nora in her efforts to keep up a good appearance. Yes, there is a certain amount of vanity about it which offends Bessie in particular, who describes Nora as a 'little overdressed throllop' *[Act I, 557]*, but Bessie's reaction is not difficult to understand. Both Mrs. Gogan and Bessie display a certain amount of vanity as they try to outboast each other in their arguments in Acts I and II. As with Nora, their vanity is part and parcel of their pride and their self-respect. Peter and Fluther's boasting and posturing is also symptomatic of their vanity, and The Covey is so vain that he regards himself as a cut above everybody else when it comes to intelligence.

Vanity as an obsession

It is when we come to Clitheroe, Brennan, Langon and those taking part in the Rising that vanity is seen as a sick and dangerous obsession. There is every reason to believe that Clitheroe at least is motivated purely from vanity. He is accused of this by Mrs. Gogan and Nora in Act I. Mrs. Gogan tells us how, when Clitheroe thought he was to be promoted 'he bought a Sam Browne belt, an' was always puttin' it on an' standin' at th' door showing it off' *[195]*. As Clitheroe makes ready to leave for the political demonstration, Nora warns him that 'Your vanity'll be th' ruin of you an' me yet. . . .' *[892]*. Clitheroe's actions would tend to confirm Nora and Mrs. Gogan's words. It is, after all, only when he learns of his promotion that he returns to the Citizen Army.

O'Casey is implying that the Rising was a war of pride and vanity. If only men such as Clitheroe could recognise the damage their actions have wrought on the community and accept that there is nothing glorious or heroic either in killing or dying in this way.

DEFINING THE PLAY

It is hard to think of another twentieth-century dramatist capable of the breadth of sympathy, range of tone, and truth to life in all its contradictory aspects, that O'Casey displays here. If the term 'tragi-comedy' means anything, this is its modern summit, because he touches extreme points both of pain and of hilarity and somehow fuses the two together into a single experience.

(Benedict Nightingale)

The Plough defies simple definition. Because it reflects the real world in all its complexity, it is possible to attach a variety of labels to the play. This section deals specifically with the terms 'tragedy' and 'comedy' as they relate to the play. Later we will deal with important dramatic features of the play.

Tragi-comedy

Although O'Casey describes *The Plough* as a 'tragedy', it is commonly agreed that the play is in fact a tragi-comedy, which is to say that it combines elements of both tragedy and comedy in such an intricate manner that, strictly speaking, it is a cross between the two. The idea of tragi-comedy is to unsettle the spectator by alternating comedy and seriousness. Tragi-comedy normally lacks the intense seriousness of tragedy and the lightheartedness of comedy. It could be argued, for instance, that because no one of the characters in the play qualifies as a truly tragic figure, in the classical sense of the word (see below), the play cannot be truly described as tragic. Likewise, it could be argued that, because of the underlying serious issues of the play, the fact that families are torn asunder and principal characters are killed, it could not possibly contain the qualities of true comedy. In order to fully appreciate the play as a tragi-comedy, it is therefore necessary to understand what constitutes both tragedy and comedy.

Tragedy

The term 'tragedy' has its origins in the classical theatre of ancient Greece. Tragic drama traditionally depicted the fall of kings and princes. It was argued that only the fall of a great man or woman could excite pity and fear, while the fall of an ordinary man, instead of being awe-inspiring, was merely pathetic. But whereas classical and Elizabethan critical theory insisted that tragedy must show the fall of great men or women, the new drama of the late nineteenth century began to challenge such notions. All men and women, regardless of birth, class or rank, were now regarded as proper subjects of drama. The traditional hero, the king, was replaced by the man-on-the-street, and the traditonal language of drama—poetry—was replaced by a careful reproduction of common speech. Tragedy still concerned characters placed in intolerable circumstances, fighting against insurmountable odds; it retained the inevitable unhappy ending; it retained the idea of the tragic hero or heroine, gaining wisdom or insight as a result of his or her suffering; and if the character was no longer one of nobility, he or she was seen to be ennobled through suffering.

Applying 'tragedy' to 'The Plough'

The Plough does confirm to *some* of those later, more general, notions of tragedy, but not all. For this reason it cannot be described as a real 'tragedy' in dramatic terms. The characters of the play are ordinary people struggling to survive poverty and hardship, and in this sense they are fighting against insurmountable odds. There is an unhappy, cruel ending: Clitheroe is killed in action; Mollser is dead and Nora's child is stillborn; Bessie is accidentally killed while helping Nora from the window; and Nora herself is virtually insane. But despite all of this, no one character is seen to have gained wisdom or insight. Even in Act III, when Nora is still sensible to what is going on about her, her stature as a character is never increased. She simply cannot accept that circumstances cannot be reversed, that Clitheroe has to act as he does given that Langon is crying out for his help. Were Nora to sympathise with her husband's dilemma, despite her own needs, then, and only then, could we speak in terms of her as a 'tragic figure'. What happens to her is tragic, but she herself is not a strong enough character to be tragic.

Bessie is a heroine, but the fact that her death is accidental, that given a choice she would probably not have gone to the window, and that Bessie does not undergo any great transformation during the play, also means that we cannot describe her as a truly 'tragic heroine'.

Similarly, Clitheroe's death, as with Mollser's, is more pathetic than it is tragic. Unlike Bessie and Nora, Clitheroe does come to learn something, he does admit that it would have been better if he'd not left Nora in the first place. But this leaves too many unanswered questions when we come to question Clitheroe's motivation. If he is admitting that he was wrong to ever become involved in the Rising, and that, painful though it might now be, he has to accept the consequences of his actions, then there is the argument in favour of his being described as a 'tragic character'. But the manner in which he abandons Nora at this point in Act III, after Nora has told him she searched for him at the barricades all night, suggests that Clitheroe's vanity is the real force behind his actions. O'Casey's stage notes are relevant here also, '(*in fear her action would give him future shame*). What possessed you to make a show of yourself, like that? . . . What way d'ye think I'll feel when I'm told my wife was bawlin' for me at th' barricades?' *[613]*. To die out of vanity is not to die a noble, tragic death.

The remaining characters in the play are very much the same people we met in Act I. There is nothing remotely tragic about The Covey and Uncle Peter. Mrs. Gogan has had to suffer the death of her child, but it is a death she is more than capable of taking in her stride, we are told she is 'a little proud of the importance of being directly connected with death' *[Act IV, 384]*. Fluther is still drinking and still bragging by the final act.

Comedy

Comedy is normally considered the opposite of tragedy. It can be used to undermine those whose behaviour has become fixed or obsessive (Uncle Peter and Mrs. Gogan are most typical of this): characters possessed by avarice or pride or sloth, and other such vices. In its concern for human wholeness, comedy often carries with it an anarchic, anti-authoritarian quality, and it can use this to expose the contradictions and inconsistencies of society's institutions as well as its individuals. *The Plough* combines a number of different types of comedy ranging from what are known as 'low' forms such as 'slapstick', 'farce', through the more subtle forms of 'verbal' and 'satirical'. (The use of 'irony' as a comic device is discussed in the chapter on 'Other Important Features of *The Plough*'.)

Slapstick

As the word suggests, slapstick is a purely physical form of knock-about comedy most often associated with circus or pantomine characters. Examples of slapstick are to be found in Acts I and II and parts of Act III. Uncle Peter chasing after The Covey with a sword in Act I or, in their second argument, the way Peter is seen to 'leap to his feet in a whirl of rage' *[676]*, and hysterically 'lifting a cup to fling at The Covey' *[681]*.

In Act II, Uncle Peter is once more treated as a clown as Mrs. Gogan leaves him holding the child and he has to chase after her with it. The two quarrels, between Bessie and Mrs. Gogan and between Fluther and The Covey, are also typical examples of slapstick. We need only look at the stage directions to see this: 'Bessie (with a push of her hand that sends Peter tottering to the end of the shop)' *[406]*; 'Mrs. Gogan (to Bessie, standing before her in a fighting attitude)' *[424]*; 'Barman (coming from behind the counter, getting between the women, and proceeding to push them towards the door)' *[429]*; 'Fluther (with his face stuck into the face of The Covey)' *[579]*; 'Barman (running from behind the counter and catching hold of The Covey)' *[600]*.

In Act III, the looting gives rise to a great deal of slapstick as the characters come and go with sacks of flour and ham, barrels of whiskey, shoes, tables and chairs. At one point, Mrs. Gogan tells Uncle Peter to 'Get up in th' prambulator an' we'll wheel you down' *[425]*, and often a production will actually have Peter do this, though O'Casey does not specify whether or not he does climb on board. The argument over the pram gives occasion for a great deal of slapstick as each woman pulls the pram back to herself; in practice this scene usually involves the two women clambering over the pram and trying to push one another off. It is a routine taken almost directly out of a circus.

Farce

Farce and slapstick often go hand in hand. The characters of farce find themselves in awkward situations, lose items of clothing and suffer physical assault, though they do not suffer too heavily. They usually have a curious childish innocence, a lack of awareness of other people's concerns and a total obsession with their own. We laugh at them while envying their capacity to ignore life's trials and tribulations. As a play, *The Plough* is not a farce, but aspects of Uncle Peter, The Covey, Fluther and Mrs. Gogan's characters and their behaviour clearly fit into this framework: Uncle Peter's childish behaviour; The Covey's obsession with socialism and '*Jenersky's Thesis on the Origin, Development, an' Consolidation of th' Evolutionary Idea of the Proletariat*'; Mrs. Gogan's curiosity and her

75

fascination with death; the fact that Fluther is such an amiable character despite the circumstances of his life and his drinking problem.

Verbal comedy

There are numerous types of verbal comedy in the play, the most direct being straightforward witticisms, such as Fluther's line in Act I: 'I think we ought to have as great a regard for religion as we can, so as to keep it out of as many things as possible' *[304]*; or again at the end of Act II when he tells Rosie that 'I hit a man last week, Rosie, an' he's fallin' yet!' *[625]*; or when, in Act III, Fluther tells the Woman from Rathmines that 'I have to go away, ma'am, to thry an' save a few things from th' burnin' buildin's' *[351]*; or Mrs. Gogan's description of Uncle Peter in Act I in his Forester's costume as '. . . Like somethin' you'd pick off a Christmas Tree' *[181]*; though The Covey's description is perhaps better again—'Lookin' like th' illegitimate son of an illegitimate child of a corporal in th' Mexican army!' *[Act I, 687]*.

Another technique O'Casey uses is repetition, in which a particular word or expression becomes funny through repeated use. The most memorable of these is Fluther's 'derogatory' and 'vice versa', and the title of The Covey's favourite book by 'Jenersky'.

The manner in which characters such as Bessie or Mrs. Gogan in particular deliver huge chunks of meandering dialogue is also a particularly striking example of verbal comedy. Any one of the women's speeches during their argument in Act II would be an example of this, or Mrs. Gogan's lengthy description of her dream in Act III, in which she imagined Fluther's death *[116-130]*.

Often the type of language misused or mispronounced is in itself comical. Examples of such are legion: 'upperosity' for expensive tastes, 'foostherin' for fussing, 'conspichuous' for conspicuous, 'in seculo seculorum' for the Latin *saecula saeculorum* (i.e. forever), 'cunundhrums' for conundrums, 'disbelieve' for I don't believe, 'wurum' for worm, 'rievin' for reefing, 'varmint' for vermin.

The verbal comedy of the play, though, is predominantly ironic. What various characters say usually contrasts sharply with the reality of the situation. We laugh at Uncle Peter and Fluther's boasts, their promises and pledges because they so obviously lack any credibility. For all The Covey's talk of socialism, he constantly insults everybody. Mrs. Gogan and Bessie Burgess defend their good names in Act II and III, but they also end up brawling like cats in Act II, and looting in Act III.

Satire

The Plough is often described as a satire on the Rising; this is true only to a certain degree. If we consider satire as a means of ridiculing vice or folly, of lampooning individuals, of censuring and protesting while still entertaining, then the play certainly fits into this category. We have already seen how the story of the Clitheroe family's disintegration parallels the way in which the city itself is torn asunder (see 'Structure', page 11). It is in this respect that the play can be said, overall, to be a satire. But because the play is actually set in the same period it is supposedly satirising, it is not purely a satire. Normally the story (or allegory) of a satire is placed in an altogether different context, such as in George Orwell's novel *Animal Farm*, for example, or Swift's *Gulliver's Travels*.

LANGUAGE

> *But there are many reasons why we treasure the plays of O'Casey. One is the way in which he (like Synge) gave voice to people who could express their feelings with awesome directness. It is no accident that both playwrights discovered this among the poor, the oppressed, the dispossessed.*
>
> *(Thomas Kilroy, programme note 1980)*

Dramatic Language

O'Casey uses dramatic language in a variety of ways and for a variety of reasons (we have just examined the use he makes of it for 'verbal comedy'). His first concern is to establish that these people are speaking as real lower-working-class Dublin people would have spoken. Unless he succeeds in doing this, his characters will not seem convincing. All of the characters, with the exception of the Speaker in Act II and the Woman from Rathmines in Act III, share a strong Dublin accent or dialect. This dialect is rich in imagery, peculiar turns of phrase and rhetoric, which gives it a distinctive, often lyrical, quality. But we can also find a large number of instances when, in order to create a particular mood, the dialogue is more akin to poetry than ordinary conversation.

Criticisms

In fact, *The Plough* is often criticised for using language which is too 'poetic' and unnatural, that O'Casey's characters speak an awkward, unreal language. At times it *is* awkward, often it *is* unreal, and his characters do regularly speak lines of poetry. But then, dramatic dialogue is never an exact replicate of the spoken word, even when it seems to be. And it must also be remembered that the play is not totally 'naturalistic' (see next section). When Uncle Peter, for example, seems to use an excess of 'alliteration' (see below), it is because he is more of a caricature than a character as we discussed under the 'farce' section above. The same applies to Mrs. Gogan, and to Fluther to a lesser degree. It is easy to accept the way in which comical figures such as these use an exaggerated language because it matches certain of their exaggerated personality traits. But when we come to Nora and Clitheroe, who are very much serious, natu-ralistic characters, then O'Casey's dialogue often fails to convince. The love scene between Nora and Clitheroe in Act I, with lines like 'little, little red-lipped Nora!' *[736]* and *[786]*, and 'turnin' a tendher sayin' into a meanin' o' malice an' spite!' *[748]*, or, later on in the same act, as they argue Nora shouts '. . . your little red-lipped Nora can go on sittin' here, makin' a companion of th' loneliness of th' night!' *[895]*. These and many more of Nora's lines sound too contrived, too artificial, when they are meant to sound like natural speech. Parts of Nora's dialogue in Act III suffer from the same malady. Take, for example, the following speech:

Nora.   Oh, I know that wherever he is, he's thinkin' of wantin' to be with me. I know he's longin' to be passin' his hand through me hair, to be caressin' me neck, to fondle me hand an' to feel me kisses clingin' to his mouth . . . *[199]*

This is awkward, artificial and embarrassingly bad dialogue, as is the following example from the same act a few moments later: 'only th' blossoms that grew out of our lives are before me now; shakin' their colours before me face, an' breathin' their sweet scent on every thought springin' up in me mind. . . .' *[225]*. When, in Act IV, Nora is insane and we hear her speak lines similar to this, they are credible precisely because she *is* insane, but here in Act III, Nora still has all her faculties.

Bearing these considerations in mind, the following is a breakdown of the various elements characteristic of O'Casey's dramatic language.

Dialect

Because the characters speak with Dublin accents, they pronounce words and form sentences in a way peculiar to Dublin people. Note, for instance, how the 'g' at the ends of words is dropped, or how 'of' becomes 'o', how 'would' becomes 'ud', how words like 'trying' are spelt 'thryin' ' with a 'h' in order to capture the exact pronunciation. Examples of dialect such as these abound, with words and phrases such as 'wather', 'wance', 'oul', 'two gems', 'mot', 'folleyed' and 'kep'. There are words which are peculiar to Dublin, such as 'ball o' malt' for whiskey, 'chiselur' for child, 'blatherin' for

78

foolish talk, 'puss' for face, 'lowser' for despicable person, 'mits' for fists, 'bowsey' for bully, 'cur' for worthless person, 'hussy' for worthless woman, 'get his goat' for annoy.

Poetic Language

In one sense, all drama is potentially poetic since it communicates, in a condensed form, strong feelings and emotions. Strictly speaking, the language of 'poetic drama' should sound like poetry, using the same heightened language and unusual rhythms we normally associate with poetry. Because, on the whole *The Plough* is a naturalistic play (see next chapter), it tends to use the common rhythms and language of everyday speech. But there are, nevertheless, instances in which characters use elements of what can only be described as poetic language.

Imagery and similes

Much of the language used by the characters in the play is rich in imagery and similes, mostly visual: Nora's description in Act I of The Covey and Peter as 'a pair o' fightin' cocks!' *[475]*; Rosie's description in Act II, of the men marching in the streets, 'You'd think they were th' glorious company of th' saints an' th' noble army of martyrs thrampin' through th' streets of paradise' *[34]*; Fluther's description in Act II of the Speaker's words 'patterin' on th' people's head, like rain fallin' on th' corn' *[104]*; The Covey's description in Act II of Uncle Peter as looking 'like green accoutred figures gone asthray out of a toyshop!' *[318]*; Brennan's description, in Act III, of the tenement folk as 'slum lice' *[531]*; Fluther's description of the door he has just fixed in Act I as 'Openin' an' shuttin' now with a well-mannered motion, like a door of a select bar in a high-class pub' *[508]*; or his assurance to Nora a moment later that he is off the drink for good, '. . . you'd have as much chance o' movin' Fluther as a tune on a tin whistle would move a deaf man an' he dead' *[536]*.

Bessie's use of biblical language includes many images, such as her description, at the end of Act I, of the rebels as 'th' lice is crawlin' about feedin' on th' fatness o' the land!' *[955]*, or in Act III as 'A lot o' vipers. . . .' *[250]*, or 'shelter me safely in th' shadow of Thy wings!' *[Act III, 740]*, or 'let patience clip away th' heaviness of th' slow-movin' hours' *[Act IV, 233]*.

But imagery is used in a much more consciously poetic way by the Speaker outside the bar in Act II. 'Bloodshed' is said to be a 'cleansing and sanctifying thing' *[58]*, as water might be in the sacrament of baptism. Later in his speech, he likens bloodshed to 'red wine' *[125]*, in which he uses the image of Jesus's blood being

79

sacrificed in the form of the Eucharist. And 'War', we are told, must be welcomed as if it were 'The Angel of God!' *[340]*.

Alliteration

Alliteration is the repetition of the same consonant sound, usually at the beginning of words in a series which appear near each other, in the same line or group of lines in poetry or prose. Unfortunately O'Casey was a little too fond of using this technique and quite often it is more of an irritation than anything else. Uncle Peter is the character most given to using alliteration, especially when in a temper, though all of the characters use it at one time or another.

The following is just a very small random set of examples. 'She makes these collars as stiff with starch as a shinin' band o' solid steel!' *[Uncle Peter, Act I, 336]*; 'I suppose you'll be singin' songs o' Sion an' songs o' Tara at th' meetin', too' *[The Covey, Act I, 309]*; '. . . th' dhread o' desthruction be a few drowsy virtues . . .' *[Mrs. Gogan, Act II, 383]*; '. . . prayin' for their blindin' an' blastin' an' burnin' in th' world to come' *[Peter, Act II, 467]*; 'flutther a feather o' Fluther' *[Fluther, Act II, 521]*; '. . . as if her mind had been lost alive in madly minglin' memories of th' past . . .' *[Bessie, Act IV, 114]*.

Lyrical

The word lyric originally meant 'suitable to sing to the music of the lyre'. Today, although the word still refers to the words of a song, in writing it is meant to indicate that the words used are musical and graceful at least to a degree. The language is heightened and often intense. The speeches delivered by Fluther and Uncle Peter during the first half of Act II are good examples:

Fluther. You couldn't feel any way else at a time like this when th' spirit of a man is pulsin' to be out fightin' for th' truth with his feet thremblin' on th' way, maybe to th' gallows, an' his ears tinglin' with th' faint, far-away sound of burstin' rifle-shots that'll maybe whip th' last little shock o' life out of him that's left lingerin' in his body! *[80-86]*

Individual words such as 'pulsin', 'thremblin', 'tinglin', and 'lingerin', contribute to the lyrical quality of such a speech, but so also does its richness of sounds and images, all straining together for affect— the 'faint, far-away sound' for guns, and the 'last shock o' life' that might be 'left lingerin'.

Whenever Mrs. Gogan has an opportunity to discuss death, she usually does so using a highly lyrical language. There are many examples of this throughout the play, but her description of Fluther's imaginary death, in Act III, is the most noteworthy:

Mrs. Gogan. . . . .An', then, I heard th' murmurs of a crowd no one could see sayin' th' litany for th' dead; an' then it got so dark that nothin' was seen but th' white face of th' corpse, gleamin' like a white wather-lily floatin' on th' top of a dark lake. . . . . 'Poor Fluther, afther havin' handed in his gun at last, his shakin' soul moored in th' place where th' wicked are at rest an' th' weary cease from throublin'. *[119-130]*

Again it is the combination of words, sounds and images, a richness like that of Fluther's in the previous example, which qualifies such a speech as being lyrical.

There are many examples of short, lyrical lines also, such as Uncle Peter's description, in Act II, of the way The Covey says 'cuckoo': 'he never says it straight out, but murmurs it with curious quiverin' ripples, like variations on a flute' *[224]*; 'A man in th' pink o' health should have a holy horror of allowin' thoughts o' death to be festerin' in his mind. . . .' *[Fluther, Act I, 244].*

Rhetoric

Rhetoric, in its modern sense, is the use of language to impress and persuade without necessarily being perfectly logical. Powerful, emotive language is often rhetorical because it relies on sentiment rather than sense to convey a point.

The Speaker outside the bar

It is in this sense that the Speaker outside the bar in Act II may be said to be using rhetoric, and likewise Fluther and Uncle Peter in their reactions to his passionate words. The Speaker is saying, in effect, that war is a good thing, that it is needed every so often to somehow cleanse the world of its sins etc. But he does not say it as directly as this, since to do so would be to expose the absurdity of such a belief. Instead, he couches, or disguises, his sentiments in religious images of Christ's sacrifice on the cross. He likens the real horrors of war to that of red wine pouring onto the battle fields.

Emotive words are used also. Ireland's political dependence on England is likened to that of a slave to his master, to a loss of manhood. This again is far from accurate. Yes, there were poor people in Ireland whose working and living conditions meant they were virtually slaves to the system, but there were people in identical conditions in England as well.

If we break down the way in which the sentences are constructed, we can see how 'repetition' in the first and last speeches is used to create a mood or urgency and determination. In the first of The Speaker's speeches in Act II, the phrase *[54-60]* 'We must

81

accustom ourselves' is repeated three times; in the final speech *[657-665]*, 'they think' and 'the fools' are both repeated three times also. Many key words and phrases have to do with the idea of a celebration as opposed to an actual massacre, for example: 'glorious', 'rejoice', 'august homage', 'cleansing and sanctifying', 'redemption', 'exhilartion', 'miracles', 'red wine', 'ripens'. In effect, this is to use language as a smoke screen, and to manipulate people like Clitheroe and Brennan.

The Covey

The Covey also indulges in a form of political rhetoric, though, unlike the Speaker outside the bar, he does not use poetic language and there may be a grain of truth in what he is saying. Instead he uses a different form of rhetoric. The Covey's line in socialist jargon is rhetorical because the language he uses is ridiculously complicated. The most obvious example of this is in the title of the book he is reading, '*Jenersky's Thesis of the Origin, Development, an' Consolidation of th' Evolutionary Idea of the Proletariat*'. When language becomes this complicated, it immediately becomes suspect. The Covey clearly enjoys blinding everybody with such high-sounding language, as when he asks Fluther in Act II, 'What does Karl Marx say about th' relation of Value to th' Cost o' Production?' *[531]*, or when earlier, he tells Rosie Redmond that 'There's only one freedom for th' workin' man: conthrol o' th' means o' production, rates of exchange, an' th' means of disthribution' *[178]*. Translated into ordinary language, The Covey is trying to say that equality for all is what people should be fighting for. To cast such a basic political premise in such technical jargon is to indulge in verbal rhetoric. It is to use language to pretend that something is more complicated than it really is.

Biblical Language

Bessie is the character who at times uses a form of biblical language. This is the language of the Authorised Version of the Bible. For example, the somewhat jumbled version of Psalm 91 she delivers at the end of Act I, 'But yous'll not escape from th' arrow that flieth be night, or th' sickness that wasteth be day. . . .' *[956]*, and again at the end of Act III when she says 'Oh God, be Thou my help in time o' throuble. An' shelter me safely in th' shadow of Thy wings!' *[739]*.

Nora likewise uses a biblical idiom during Act III, as Clitheroe returns: '. . . my own Jack, that I thought was lost is found, that I thought was dead is alive again! . . . Oh, God be praised for ever, evermore!' *[545]*. Both Mrs. Gogan and Uncle Peter also use the idiom at times, but not nearly as accurately as Bessie.

82

PART 4

Other important features of 'The Plough'

O'CASEY'S WOMEN

*The most striking and the most sympathetic figures
in O'Casey's plays are usually the women. Indeed he
has written few plays without a dominant female
personality.*

(Carol Coulter, 1980)

It is important to appreciate that, by and large, O'Casey's women
are strong-willed and independent-minded, as compared with the
men who are temperamentally weak and more than ready to step in
line to accept whatever popular, romantic myths they are fed. It is
interesting, for example, that while none of the sword-swinging
boasters, i.e. Fluther and Peter, in Act II ever actually come to
blows, the women, i.e. Bessie and Mrs. Gogan, waste no time in
putting their words into action and take to the streets in a fist fight.

Women, as portrayed by O'Casey, are always the stronger, more
courageous of the sexes. Witness Mrs. Gogan's struggle to survive
with no husband and two children, or Bessie's great pride despite
being virtually destitute. Women may aspire to greater things, as,
for example, Nora does in trying to escape the tenements, but they
are never given to pretension or posturing in the way that the men
are. We can see such qualities in Nora in Act I as she tries to keep
her home together against all odds, with a husband who is more
concerned about his own heroic image than his home. In Act II,
both Bessie and Mrs. Gogan display the fighting spirit which the
men make false claim to. It is this same practical, fighting spirit
which, later in the play, becomes a positive force and drives Bessie
to help Nora in her hour of need.

Women, for the most part, are the most striking and the most
sympathetic figures in all of O'Casey's work. With the few ex-
ceptions of men like Fluther, the men are cast as pitiable, pathetic
figures.

CONSIDERING IRONY

The final act of the play contains a great deal of irony. It is useful to
remember this when we consider why it is that *The Plough* is often

described as an 'ironic' play. Much of the play's irony is set up in the previous acts and only comes into effect in the final act. There is an almost limitless number of examples, and the following is just a small sample:

1. Mollser, who told Nora in Act I that 'I do be terrible afraid I'll die sometime when I'm be meself', is indeed dead by Act IV.

2. Bessie, who, up to now, was regarded as nothing more than a quarrelsome, violent women, reveals a number of heroic qualities.

3. It is Bessie who nurses and comforts Nora, although in Act I Nora believed Bessie would one day do her harm.

4. In Act II, Clitheroe toasts a drink to 'Death for th' Independence of Ireland!' By Act IV, we realise he has not just brought about his own pathetic death but also the death of his first child and a form of mental death for Nora.

5. In Act II, the Figure in the Window says, 'Ireland has not known the exhilaration of war. . . .' What we see of war in Act IV is certainly not exhilarating.

6. In Act II, the Figure in the Window says 'Heroism has come back to the earth'. The kind of basic, humane heroism as displayed by Fluther and Bessie in Act IV proves to be far greater than any military heroism.

7. Whereas, in Act I, it was Clitheroe who sang to Nora, in Act IV it is Bessie who sings to her.

8. It is the men, including Capt. Brennan, who come to Bessie for protection, reversing the stereotype of men as protectors and women as the weaker of the sexes.

9. In Act I, Nora warns Clitheroe that 'Your vanity'll be th' ruin of you an' me yet. . . .' Act IV proves how accurate her prophecy was.

10. After Bessie is shot, Mrs. Gogan brings Nora to what was Mollser's bed, which brings to mind how envious Mollser was of Nora and all she had. Now Nora has even less than Mollser had.

Irony takes many forms, but here we can see it basically involves things being reversed in an unexpected way; contradictions or people's worst expectations actually coming to pass; it may be general, or specific, to one person; humorous, or extremely painful.

CONFLICTS

A play is built upon what are termed 'conflicts'. It is these which give dynamism to the drama by clashing together at various points. These overall conflicts are far more general than the conflicts we find between the different characters. The main points in *The Plough* are:

(1) Nationalism versus Humanitarianism

Nationalism is seen to be more concerned with glorious causes and heroic achievements on the battlefield than actually helping those in need. It is The Covey who argues for a form of concerned politics that will have concrete results, helping destitute people like Mrs. Gogan and her daughter Mollser, or Bessie Burgess.

(2) Romance versus Reality

Against a romantic view of the Rising as a great, heroic battle fought by fearless men, the play presents us with a less attractive picture of men driven more by vanity and fear than anything else, and of the Irish people attacking and mobbing the rebels as well as looting shops and bars. In general, the men are seen to be dreamers and poseurs, as opposed to the women, who are more practical and down to earth.

(3) Military Heroism versus Domestic Heroism

The modest, inconspicious acts of generosity and individual bravery are seen to be of more worth than all the efforts of those fighting and dying in the Rising. Fluther and Bessie Burgess are portrayed as typical of the real unsung heroes of the rebellion, while men like Brennan and Clitheroe are portrayed as being merely misguided and motivated by vanity more than any real sense of patriotism or loyalty.

CONTRAST, MOOD AND PACE

If we look at each act individually, we can see how the mood (i.e. the general atmosphere) and pace (i.e. the speed of the action) can alter and change. One moment there may be a mood of excitement and this may suddenly be contrasted with a mood of sadness. There may be a scene with a frantic amount of activity, in which case we say the pace is fast, which is then contrasted with a slow pace. The following rough breakdown of the mood and pace in Act I is meant as an example of just how much these elements can vary within each act and so cause a contrast.

As Act I opens, the pace is slow and there is no noticeable mood since Fluther and Mrs. Gogan are having an ordinary conversation. The mood becomes tense as Fluther argues with The Covey, and the pace speeds up as Uncle Peter chases The Covey from the room.

With Nora's entrance, order is restored and the pace slows down once again. There is a sudden contrast from a relatively friendly mood to an intense mood of fear when Bessie Burgess enters. Once more, order is restored as The Covey enters and Bessie is evicted, but yet again the pace speeds up as Peter chases The Covey from the room, and again when Clitheroe learns that Nora has concealed the news of his promotion.

DRAMATIC CLIMAX

Act III contains the high-point or 'dramatic climax' of the entire play. The Rising is now at its height and the relationship between Nora and Clitheroe is finally torn asunder. The first two acts have been building up to this dramatic climax. By the end of the Act III, the moment has already passed. The city has toppled, lives have been lost. We are now heading into the slow-paced, darker mood of the final act.

MUSICAL REFERENCES

As with all of O'Casey's plays, songs are a prominent feature of *The Plough*. These songs help to add to the colour and exuberance of the play as a whole. In Act I, The Covey taunts and provokes Uncle Peter with old patriotic songs such as, 'Dear harp o' me counthry' *[450]*, or 'Oh, where's th' slave so lowly' *[668]*. During the same act, Clitheroe sings a love song to Nora, Brennan is heard whistling 'The Soldiers Song' as Nora and Clitheroe argue, while later on, the act concludes with the sound of the Dublin Fusiliers singing 'It's a long way to Tipperary' as they march to the boat. At the end of Act II, Rosie Redmond serenades Fluther with a cheeky ballad, while at the end of the next act, Fluther sings 'For he's a jolly good fellow' to himself. At the end of Act IV, we hear the English soldiers singing the propagandist war song 'Keep the home fires burning'. Throughout the play, we also have a number of examples of Bessie Burgess singing her Anglican hymns.

MELODRAMA

The basic appeal of melodrama is to pity and fear, but these elements are greatly exaggerated so that a situation or a scene verges on the sensational. There are a number of such melodramatic moments in *The Plough*.

During Act I, when Nora begs Clitheroe not to return to the Citizen Army, her language and the general emotion of the scene

86

are melodramatic *[829 to end of act]*. In Act II, the street scene outside the bar with its cheering crowds and the emotive words of the Speaker is melodramatic. At the end of the same act, with the entrance of Clitheroe, Brennan and Lieut. Langon, once more the language and the mood of the section is melodramatic as the three men pledge themselves to the cause of Irish Independence *[634-673]*.

In Act III, much of what Nora has to say and do can be classed as melodramatic: her description of the barricades and the dead young rebel; her fight with the other women and her description of the fear she saw in the rebels' eyes. This melodrama comes to a climax with Clitheroe's entrance *[514]*. Langon is crying out for help as he lies wounded on the ground, while Nora begs Clitheroe to abandon his fellow rebels. In true melodramatic fashion, Nora faints as Clitheroe opts to carry Brennan to safety. The act also ends on a melodramatic note as the sounds of rifle shots and machine guns fill the air and Bessie runs for help.

Act IV is highly melodramatic as a whole. Mollser is dead, Nora's child is still-born, Nora herself is insane, and what is more, we learn of Clitheroe's death. So many deaths and so much pain in such a short space of time is about as melodramatic as a play can be. But Bessie's sudden, unexpected death is in itself also melodramatic.

DOMESTIC DRAMA

Domestic drama is concerned primarily with the daily problems of a typical family, i.e. family relationships, food, work and such day-to-day considerations within the home. This label clearly applies to Act I of *The Plough*, but for the rest of the play, such domestic issues are of secondary importance, and the style of the play never remains constant.

NATURALISM

This term applies to a form of drama which carefully reproduces in realistic detail scenes closely resembling that of everyday life. O'Casey goes to great pains to describe how the Clitheroes' home, Bessie's attic, the outside of the tenements and the inside of a bar should look. He describes the type of furniture, the pictures on the walls, the fireplace, positioning of doors and windows etc. We are left with the impression of actually looking into real scenes of Dublin tenement life. Likewise the characters of 'naturalistic' drama are also meant to reflect a convincing picture of real individuals living at a particular time and in a particular place. If all the characters in *The Plough* don't necessary fit into this category (Uncle Peter, for example), they do all at least approach being realistic.

But the play is not entirely naturalistic. A naturalistic play is usually expected to tell a straightforward story about a particular set of characters. The way in which *The Plough* is structured does not follow this pattern. Though we can say that the Clitheroe household is at the heart of the play, this is made far from obvious because the play is also the story of Bessie Burgess, Mrs. Gogan, and Fluther, as well as the story of the Rising with references to its leaders. This gives the play many narrative levels and tends at times to place the main emphasis on the social and political background of the play. This form of what was called 'Epic Theatre' was first championed on the continent in the early 1920s and O'Casey was influenced by it, especially in his later plays. The huge sweep of events, the assortment of odd-ball characters, the mixture of comedy and tragedy, the strong political elements to the play, all of these elements combined give *The Plough* many of the hallmarks of Epic Theatre.

PART 5

Questions

SPECIFIC QUESTIONS (PASS)

Act 1

(from line *1* to *221*)
1. From the descriptions of the Clitheroes' home, list the details that suggest an attempt is being made to make the place look 'respectable'.
2. Describe Fluther, Uncle Peter and Mrs. Gogan's physical appearance. What does O'Casey tell us about them as characters?
3. What are these three characters doing in the Clitheroes' home as the play begins?
4. During her first conversation with Fluther, what kinds of things does Mrs. Gogan tell us about other characters in the play?

(from line *222* to *381*)
5. Why has The Covey returned home from work early? Describe his physical appearance and say what this might tell us about his character.
6. What do Fluther and The Covey argue about in their first quarrel? Do they argue about more than one thing? In your opinion, does either one make more sense than the other?

(from line *382* to *462*)
7. Do you think the scene in which Mrs. Gogan, Fluther and Peter make over the picture of the 'Sleepin' Vennis' is meant to be serious or comical? Give reasons for your answer.
8. In what way/ways does Peter contradict himself during his first argument with The Covey?
9. List the number of arguments (including this one between Peter and The Covey) that have taken place up to this point in this act.

(from line *463* to *590*)
10. Describe Nora's physical appearance, including her clothes. What can we say about her character judging from these first impressions?
11. Why do you think Nora is so concerned about Peter and The Covey arguing?
12. Describe Bessie Burgess and say why it is she is so annoyed with Nora.

13. What do we learn about Bessie in the short appearance she makes here?
14. Describe Clitheroe's physical appearance.

(from line *591* to *705*)
15. Why does The Covey tell Clitheroe that the Citizen Army is 'bringin' disgrace' on the Plough and the Stars? Do you think this may be a particularly important subject in relation to the play as a whole?
16. Who starts the second fight between Peter and The Covey? Do you find these kinds of arguments comical or serious?
17. Does the 'mood' and the 'pace' of the play seem to change after Nora and Clitheroe are left alone? If so, in what way and why?

(from line *706* to end of act)
18. Is there tension between Nora and Clitheroe, and, if so, why? What do they talk about to begin with?
19. Both characters seem in some way uneasy. How does this uneasiness manifest itself?
20. Is Clitheroe right to be angry with Nora for concealing the news of his promotion? Is Nora right to be angry with Clitheroe for returning to the Citizen Army?
21. Is Nora right in accusing Clitheroe of being motivated only by 'vanity', and why is this so important a subject to the play as a whole?
22. Why is there a poignant irony in Mollser's envy of Nora?
23. What is the meaning of Bessie's final speech?

Act II

(from line *1* to *120*)
1. How much time has elapsed since the end of Act I, and what is going on outside the bar?
2. What is Rosie Redmond concerned about as the act opens?
3. What can we say about the language used by the Speaker in his first speech?
4. What kind of a mood are Fluther and Peter in as they enter the bar, and what has them this way?
5. Is there any similarity in the language used by Fluther and Peter and that used by the Speaker?

(from line *121* to *277*)
6. What is the significance of 'red wine' as an image used by the Speaker? Is there a religious connection?

7. What do you think The Covey means when he asks Rosie 'What's the use o' freedom, if it's not economic freedom'? Is this the same type of freedom as the Speaker has been talking about?
8. Do you think Rosie understands what The Covey is talking about and the kind of language he is using?
9. Why do you think Mrs. Gogan brings her baby into the bar with her?
10. Why does Peter think his pilgrimages to Bodenstown each year are so important? What does Fluther make of them?

(from line *278* to *448*)
11. Why is Bessie so concerned about 'little Catholic Belgium'?
12. In the argument that follows, Bessie and The Covey stand together on one side of the bar. What do they have in common? In what way can we say that the argument in the bar is in ironic contrast to the words of the Speaker at this point in his speech?
13. If you were to sum up what exactly it is the two women row about, what would it be—politics, religion, respectability?
14. How do Fluther and Peter react to the women fighting and in what way could this be said to be ironic?

(from line *449* to *633*)
15. What does Fluther mean by 'th' Shan Van Vok!', and what does The Covey think of it?
16. Can we believe Fluther's boasts at this point about his valour and bravery?
17. Why do you think Fluther gets so angry with The Covey before Rosie Redmond becomes involved in the argument?
18. Should we take what The Covey is saying seriously? Is he making any sense about politics?
19. What does the manner in which The Covey insults Rosie tell us about his character?
20. Why do you think Fluther is so quick to come to Rosie's defence?
21. Do you think Rosie is really impressed by Fluther's fighting powers or is she up to something?

(from line *634* to end of act)
22. What is the 'mood' of Clitheroe, Brennan and Langon as they enter the bar? How does this compare with the mood of Peter and Fluther as they entered the bar for the first time in the act?
23. In what sense is history used by the Speaker in his final speech to rouse the crowd? What other aspects of these final words are significant?
24. In the light of what happens to Clitheroe, Brennan and Langon later in the play, why are the three pledges they make, 'Death', 'Imprisonment' and 'Wounds', respectively, ironic?

Act III

(from line *1* to *135*)
1. Can we tell anything about the occupants of the tenement from the external description given to us by O'Casey?
2. What are your impressions of Mollser during the opening moments of this act?
3. How much time has passed since Act II?
4. What, according to Peter and The Covey, is happening in the city?
5. Why does Bessie sound so satisfied by the turn of events in the rebellion?
6. In what way is Mrs. Gogan's dream of Fluther's death consistent with her character?

(from line *136* to *242*)
7. Where have Fluther and Nora been, and what is Nora's state of mind?
8. What does Bessie mean by 'Stabbin' in the back the men that are dyin' in the threnches for them!'?
9. Why is it Nora fought against the other women at the barricades?
10. In what way does Nora's descriptions of a dead rebel contrast sharply with the descriptions of war given by the Speaker in Act II?

(from line *243* to *369*)
11. In what way does the mood change after Nora enters the house?
12. Is it significant that O'Casey treats the Rising comically at this point with scenes of looting and plundering by characters who earlier professed to be patriotic?

(from line *370* to *513*)
13. What is so important about the pram over which Bessie and Mrs. Gogan argue?
14. Why doesn't Peter go with the others to loot the shops, and why does he try to lock The Covey and the others out?
15. In terms of their claims to respectability, what is so ironic about Bessie and Mrs. Gogan looting the shops?

(from line *514* to *672*)
16. Why is Brennan so angry with Clitheroe as they enter carrying the wounded Lieut. Langon?
17. Why is it significant that Brennan describes the tenement people as 'slum lice'?

18. Is Nora unreasonable in expecting Clitheroe to abandon the wounded Langon and return home with her? Is she in her right senses?
19. In the light of Brennan's appearance in the final act, why is it so ironic that here it is Brennan who insists Clitheroe cannot desert his fellow soldiers?
20. Why do you think Clitheroe decides not to stay with Nora? Can we say for certain why this is or can we only guess?

(from *673* to end of act)
21. Why does it come as a surprise that Bessie is willing to risk her life for Nora, and why can Fluther not fetch a doctor for Nora?
22. What instances, if any, of 'melodrama' can you find in this act?

Act IV

(from line *1* to *128*)
1. What are the most significant differences between the Clitheroes' living quarters and those of Bessie's as described here?
2. How much time has elapsed between this and Act III?
3. Describe the scene in your own words as the act opens.
4. What has happened to Nora and Mollser?
5. What has Bessie been doing for Nora?

(from line *129* to *263*)
6. Does Brennan have more than one reason for coming here?
7. Can we believe Brennan's account of Clitheroe's death? Is it as glorious as his Commandant maintains?
8. What do you think is the attitude of the others to Brennan?
9. For Nora, is news of her husband's death joyful, as Brennan describes it?
10. What is the irony of Bessie's words of comfort to Nora that 'sorrow may endure for th' night, but joy cometh in th' mornin''?

(from line *264* to *507*)
11. Why does Fluther say that Mollser's death has Mrs. Gogan 'in her element'? Is he right?
12. What do you think is the significance of The Covey's line to Stoddart that more people die of consumption than are killed in wars?
13. What does Mrs. Gogan tell us about what Fluther did for her, and what does she say about Bessie's treatment of Mollser?
14. Why does Bessie react so angrily to being described by Stoddart as a 'Shinner'?

15. What is the mood of Fluther, The Covey and Peter as they return after having brought Mollser's coffin out?
16. Between this point and the beginning of the play, can we say that any of the characters have changed in any way?

(from line *508* to the end)
17. Where does Nora think she is when she enters for the second time?
18. Why is it so ironic that Bessie should be shot in place of Nora?
19. Why does Nora not seem to hear Bessie's pleas for help?
20. Where does Mrs. Gogan take Nora to, and why is this so ironic?
21. Is there any optimism to be found as the final act comes to a conclusion?

* * *

The following set of questions on the play are taken from a previous Leaving Certificate Pass paper (1989). The extract in question, which was printed in full, was from Act I, lines 820 to 920 (line references are from the Gill and Macmillan edition of the play).

Having read the extract, answer one of the following questions, 1, 2, or 3.

1.(a)(i) What view of Nora do you derive from the above extract?
   (ii) How does this compare with your view of Nora based on the play as a whole?
  (b) The interests of home in conflict with the interests of country is a central theme in *The Plough and the Stars*. Discuss, with the aid of suitable quotation or reference, how this theme is treated throughout the play.

2.(a) In what way can the above extract be regarded as a key scene in the play?
  (b) '. . . you'll make a glorious cause of what you're doin',' Nora says to her husband. Do you think that *The Plough and the Stars* portrays war as glorious? Support your answer by reference or quotation.

3.   'As well as portraying the misery of their lives, O'Casey finds much that is humorous in his characters.' Discuss this view of *The Plough and the Stars*, supporting your points by relevant quotation or reference.

GENERAL DISCUSSION QUESTIONS (HONOURS)

1. The main characters of O'Casey's play show a number of important contradictions. Give a number of examples of such contradictions and say what effect they have on the characters in question.

2. Discuss O'Casey's use of comedy and tragedy in *The Plough*. Give examples of each in your answer.

3. *The Plough and the Stars* has often been described as an ironic play. What does this mean? Support your answer with examples and quotations.

4. 'In *The Plough and the Stars*, O'Casey demonstrates the power of language. It is a case of the pen being mightier than the sword.' Discuss.

5. 'O'Casey's version of the Easter Rising is one-sided, prejudiced and unfair on those who took part in the fighting.' Say whether you feel there might be some truth to this statement, with reference to events and characters in the play.

6. 'Great plays never have and never will be written about hate. They are written about reconciliation and forgiveness.' Discuss whether or not *The Plough* is a play about 'hate' or about 'reconciliation and forgiveness.'

7. '*The Plough* offers no political solutions. Instead it attacks and undermines all forms of politics.' Discuss with relevant quotations and references.

8. Explain the significance of the play's title and its relevance to the play as a whole.

9. 'O'Casey's men have very little to recommend themselves. They are selfish, glory-seeking posers. His women are the real heroes because of their inherent humanity and compassion, and because they, in the end, are the ones to suffer most.' Discuss.

10. 'Against the abstract idealism and romantic outlook of those who led the Easter Rising, O'Casey sets the humanity of those who lived in the tenements.' Discuss.

11. O'Casey wrote: 'We should, however, be careful of well-meaning idealism; good as it may be and well-meaning, its flame in a few hearts may not give them new life and new hope to the many, but dwindle into ghastly and futile funeral pyres in which many are uselessly destroyed and enormous damage done to all.' Discuss how O'Casey actually tries to demonstrate this in *The Plough*.

12. 'The essence of *The Plough and the Stars*, and the core of its wider appeal beyond wider shores, is its celebration of the terror and pity of revolution.' Discuss how it is that we can find both 'terror' and 'pity' in *The Plough*.

13. 'No real character can be put in a play unless some of the reality is taken out of him through the heightening, widening and deepening of the character by the dramatist who created him.' Discuss this statement of O'Casey's with reference to *The Plough*.

14. Should we regard *The Plough* as a purely negative play with very little in the way of hope or optimism?

15. We can find at least four principal facets to O'Casey as a writer—the lyric, the caustic, the playful and the sombre. Discuss these aspects in relation to *The Plough*, giving example of and references to each.

16. 'O'Casey's characters rarely succumb to doom and gloom, although circumstances often push them in this direction. First and foremost, they are survivors.' Discuss.

17. Is the message of *The Plough* simply anti-war or is it more complicated than this?

18. In your opinion, what are the most 'dramatic' or 'tense' scenes of *The Plough*, and what are the weakest, if any?

19. List what you feel to be the primary conflicts in the play and describe these in your own words with suitable reference and quotation.

20. Describe the ways in which different characters in *The Plough* use different types of language, turns of phrase, quotations and dialect.

The following two questions are from the 1989 Honours Leaving Certificate paper.

1. 'Fluther Good is a braggart, a clown and a drunkard, but he is also a man of courage and a sympathetic human being.' Discuss this view, supporting your answer by relevant quotation from or reference to *The Plough and the Stars*.

or

2. 'O'Casey's *The Plough and the Stars* is essentially a satire on patriotism and on war.' Discuss this view, supporting your answer by quotation or reference.